The Picnic Book

The Black Moth

Carol Wright

The Picnic Book

Illustrations by Graham Percy

HART-DAVIS, MACGIBBON
GRANADA PUBLISHING
London Toronto Sydney New York

Published by Granada Publishing in
Hart-Davis, MacGibbon Ltd 1978

Granada Publishing Limited
Frogmore, St Albans, Herts AL2 2NF
and
3 Upper James Street, London W1R 4BP
1221 Avenue of the Americas, New York, NY 10020 USA
117 York Street, Sydney, NSW 2000, Australia
100 Skyway Avenue, Toronto, Ontario, Canada M9W 3A6
Trio City, Coventry Street, Johannesburg 2001, South Africa

Copyright © Carol Wright 1978

ISBN 0 246 10998 X

Printed in Great Britain by
Richard Clay (The Chaucer Press) Ltd
Bungay, Suffolk
Set in Linotype Times

Acknowledgements

The author would like to thank the many hosts and tolerant co-participators on memorable picnics in many parts of the world from the sunny beaches of Porto Santo island to the Canadian Rockies. And those who have tested out recipes and ideas; not least my husband who has survived many a car-borne picnic abroad. Also Dawn Willis for typing the manuscript and to the following for helping with recipes, information and ideas: the New Zealand Lamb Information Bureau, Pasta Bureau, Flour Advisory Bureau, Danish and German Food Centres, Spanish Olive Information Bureau, Taunton Cider Company, Kraft and Stork Margarine Kitchens, Thermos Limited and Cross Paperware Limited.

METRIC WEIGHTS AND MEASURES

g = gram; kg = kilogram; ml = millilitre;

Exact equivalents	Approximate equivalents	Metric cookery
	$\frac{1}{2}$ oz = 15g	
1oz = 28.3g	1oz = 30g	1oz = 25g
4oz = 113.4g	4oz = 120g	4oz = 100–125g
8oz = 226.8g	8oz = 240g	8oz = 225g
1lb = 453.6g	1lb = 480g	1lb = 450g
2.2lb = 1kg	2$\frac{1}{4}$lb = 1kg	2–2$\frac{1}{4}$lb = 1kg

* * *

	$\frac{1}{8}$pt (2$\frac{1}{2}$ fl oz) = 75ml	
$\frac{1}{4}$pt = 142ml	$\frac{1}{4}$pt (5 fl oz) = 150ml	$\frac{1}{4}$pt = 125–150ml
$\frac{1}{2}$pt = 284ml	$\frac{1}{2}$pt (10 fl oz) = 275ml	$\frac{1}{2}$pt = 250–275ml
$\frac{3}{4}$pt = 426ml	$\frac{3}{4}$pt (15 fl oz) = 425ml	$\frac{3}{4}$pt = 400–425ml
1pt = 568ml	1pt (20 fl oz) = 575ml	1pt = 500–575ml
1$\frac{3}{4}$pt = 0.994 litre	1$\frac{3}{4}$pt (35 fl oz) = 1 litre	1$\frac{3}{4}$pt = 900ml

Note: The left-hand column is purely for reference. The centre column is for doing quick conversions; the equivalents are accurate enough for practical cookery purposes, as grams and millilitres are so small that plus or minus five makes very little difference. The right-hand column shows the amounts generally used in metric cookery, where 25g is used instead of 1oz, and 25ml instead of 1 fl oz. This produces a dish which is slightly smaller, but still has the correct proportion of solids to liquids.

Contents

1

Pleasure Parties

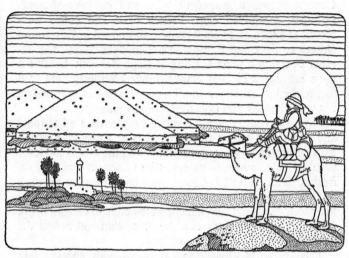

'What's inside it?' asks the Mole, greedily eyeing a picnic hamper in *The Wind in the Willows*.

'Coldtonguecoldhamcoldbeefpickledgherkinssaladfrench-rollscresssandwidgespottedmeatgingerbeerlemonadesoda-water –' the Rat begins.

'Oh, stop, stop!' cries ecstatic Mole. 'This is too much!' and so begins a riverside picnic that expresses the ultimate in happy picnic imagery – a cool summer stream, gently nodding trees and plentiful food, succulent and easy to eat ...

Unfortunately the real thing can fall somewhat short of Kenneth Grahame's idyll, and though a picnic, according to the *Concise Oxford Dictionary*, is 'a pleasure party including a meal out of doors' many a one has turned out to be more reminiscent of *Three Men in a Boat*, that catalogue of culinary and other disasters. Those mishaps sprang partly

1

from having the wrong kinds of provisions, and one of the aims of this book is to present ideas for outdoor meals that are easy to prepare and carry and easy to eat even in less-than-ideal conditions.

I have been lucky enough to enjoy many kinds of picnic from the very simple to the lavish. My biggest was one in Canada at which grapefruit juice and gin 'eye-openers', sausages, scrambled eggs, French toast and coffee were served at 6.00 a.m. to 6000 people, all dressed in Edwardian clothes to celebrate Edmonton's 'Klondyke Days'. On another occasion a press briefing at Cape Kennedy became a lawn eat-out, with cold chicken and deliciously cold iced tea. In the United States, too, I have breakfasted *al fresco* on hot waffles, steak and eggs during a morning ride.

But my favourite picnic is much simpler than all of these and one that I repeat regularly. It is at Cape St Vincent, Europe's most south-westerly point, and the fare is modest: buttered rolls, whole tomatoes, sliced ham, cheese chunks, fresh fruit and a bottle of local red wine. From the car park in front of the white squat lighthouse, I climb down off the flat windy headland into a niche in the cliffs to eat and drink while I watch the birds and the ships that toil round the headland.

This is the ideal way to eat out – with unfussy fare that's nourishing, thirst-quenching, easy to assemble and eat. But in these days of cling wrap, plastic self-seal boxes, foil and chiller bags it's possible to take along more elaborate food without investing in a lot of expensive gear. The average kitchen should contain all the essentials for a successful picnic of any kind.

The basic check list for a quick getaway should include:

Plates, cups, saucers, bowls
Cutlery
A sharp knife
Serving spoons
Paper napkins or roll of kitchen paper
Corkscrew, bottle opener, tin opener
Salt, pepper, sugar, mustard
Board or tray for slicing and serving food

Damp flannel in a plastic bag, small hand towel
Stain-removal kit
First aid kit with insect repellent
Some large plastic bags for rubbish, dirty crocks etc,
    with wire ties to seal when full
Bottle of cold water
Rug or ground sheet

Wrapping materials are needed, of course. Cling wrap is fine for sandwiches and for keeping ready-buttered bread and rolls clean and fresh. Salads and cold meats, pre-set on plates, can be covered with cling wrap for travelling. Plastic bags are excellent for carrying salad stuffs – but never mix salads with dressing before leaving home or they will go brown and soggy; take the dressing along in a bottle. Mayonnaise, unless home made, will separate out on a hot day and should also be kept apart until needed.

Deep-freeze suppliers are excellent sources of plastic boxes of all sizes, round or square, which are perfect for picnics. Prawn cocktails can be placed in them; mousses sweet or savoury; or jellies, blancmanges and trifles can be put to set in them safely. A picnic cake (see page 47) can be cooked and carried in a foil tray, and foil trays can also be used for carrying cold meats and salads. A roll of kitchen foil is a boon for the picnic maker. It wraps closely and cleanly round foods like bread, sandwiches, biscuits and cake. Salt and pepper can be carried in twists of foil. Empty yogurt and cream cartons can be used for individual fruit mousses and other desserts. Plastic margarine tubs can also be saved for picnic use and make good butter containers.

For serving the food paper plates are good in that they need no washing up, but they do tend to bend when balanced on one's knees. Plastic plates are better if china is too heavy to carry. The essential of every picnic is to have something flat to eat off. Only a professional juggler can balance a tea cup in an average bumpy field. A fold-up table is useful, but best are the airline-style plastic trays with recesses for different dishes, a place to stand a glass, and a rigid base from which to work. If you cannot find these in the shops, buy enough small round or square trays in tin or rigid plastic, one for each picnicker, preferably with deep rims to prevent spills.

Individual lunch boxes are fine for finger food, and children love having their own. In fact, an idea for a smaller children's party is to take the picnic theme indoors and sit the kids on the floor, each with his own surprise food box. It saves a lot of hassle.

Taking drinks to picnics is more fully covered in Chapter 10, but though it's possible to do without special chiller boxes or flasks, investment in two or three vacuum flasks with wide necks is worth while, and it's not necessary to keep the flask at the back of cupboard just for that sunny day outing. A vacuum flask kept near the stove can save on fuel bills. Surplus boiled water can be kept hot in it for cooking vegetables, and at night the early morning cup of tea or coffee can be prepared and put in it. Soups can be kept hot for late-comers as can second servings, also casseroles and other dishes.

On picnics flasks can be used for hot or cold items – for keeping casseroles, stews and soups hot, as shown in the Meals in a Mug chapter, and for keeping cool butter, ice, drinks, jellies, fruit salads and mousses.

Ideal for carrying foods and bottles are the deep insulated bags with ice packs which are chilled in the fridge until needed (or can be boiled to help keep foods hot in transit) and in which a lot of food can be packed and carried easily. The bags have plastic linings which can be sponged clean after use.

Vacuum flasks probably offer the easiest way of having hot food at the picnic, but they're not such fun as building your own fire and cooking over it. It is the lovely, messy childhood dream eating half cooked, indigestible food, eyes kippered from cooking, and afterwards scrubbing all that grimy black carbon from the pan bottoms.

It's far better to take along a small portable charcoal-burning barbecue or a camping gas stove with wind shield that can easily be set up in a sheltered spot for boiling water and cooking simple frying-pan meals.

The town dweller's wish to visit the countryside and enjoy a meal amidst fields and woods has been recognised by the

Countryside Commission, a non-profit body that presents the countryside to town people as a recreation area – but one which can be enjoyed in harmony by both farmer and visitor. The townee too often sees the farmer as the man who closes fields to picnickers while the farmer see the picnicker as a person who leaves gates open, tramples crops and deposits broken bottles which injure animals. The Commission has done a lot of work to promote understanding between the two sides, creating open days and permanent 'farm trails' so that visitors can learn something about modern farming while enjoying a day in the country, walking the trail and picnicking.

Picnicking carries responsibilities, and even Mole found the end of his picnic a little tedious : 'Packing the basket was not quite such pleasant work as unpacking the basket. It never is. But the Mole was bent on enjoying everything and although just when he had got the basket packed and strapped up rightly he saw a plate staring up at him from the grass, and when the job had been done again, the Rat pointed out a fork which anybody ought to have seen, and last of all, behold the mustard pot, which he had been sitting on without knowing it.' The Country Code, drawn up in 1951, is down to earth on picnics and applicable anywhere. Its basic points are :

Leave no litter. Cans and broken bottles injure livestock. Bags and wrappers can choke animals to death. Guard against fire risks and be careful with cigarettes, matches and broken glass which can concentrate heat on to grass or leaves to create a fire; it takes fifty years for some trees to grow to maturity and the thoughtless flick of a cigarette end or the knocking out of a pipe can destroy generations of forest. (Australians, used to bush fires, say succinctly : 'One flaming match, no flaming trees.')

Fasten any gates that you open. Keep your dog under control (over 4000 sheep a year in Britain are killed by marauding dogs – about £30,000 worth). Avoid damaging fences, hedges and walls, and keep to paths when crossing farm land, for what looks like long grass to a visitor may be a valuable crop. Don't pollute water supplies and do drive carefully on country roads where animals may be on the move. In general protect wild life, wild plants and trees. Carving your initials on a tree is no longer romantic; a dead tree is unsuitable for trysts.

Though it may be fun to add a few seasonable blackberries or wild nuts to the *al fresco* feast, small children should not be allowed on berry safaris on their own. It's as well to take a small wild-flower book with lists of poisonous varieties so that children can learn something of wild life.

If a child at a picnic does eat something poisonous, likely symptoms are doublng up with violent stomach pains, vomiting or developing diarrhoea. Others are burning throat, dry mouth, excessive thirst, high temperature and hot, dry skin. The child may be restless or drowsy, with dizziness, cramp or headaches. If there's any suspicion of poisoning, take the child directly to the nearest hospital emergency department, if possible with a piece of the suspect plant for identification.

2
Up and Away

Hastiest is often happiest where picnics are concerned. The best are those that are spontaneously born on the road. Touring in a foreign country or just out for a drive, suddenly the day seems exactly right and there's a foray to the nearest shops. France is probably the best country for this. I remember, on a dull and drizzly February Sunday, driving out to Fontainebleau, south of Paris. Deciding that the restaurants would be crowded with Sunday diners, and nursing too much *vin* very *ordinaire* from the night before, we opted for the open air.

In the suburbs we collected slices of quiche, a baton of bread, freshly made spiced sausage, a little coleslaw, thinly sliced smoked ham, some creamy cheese and fruit; we bought paper napkins and cups at a newsagent's and a bottle of champagne. We made for the Chaos, a kind of naturally created confusion of massive rocks balanced among

7

tall thin trees, and while the rain dripped from the branches we ate a delicious lunch half in, half out of the car.

Champagne, or any sparkling wine, is the perfect drink for an instant picnic as it needs no corkscrew and gives the slightest meal a sense of occasion. The purist may blench at champagne from cardboard cups, but he's privileged. Champagne from a tooth mug is all right for me. I've even drunk it from the bottle on the banks of the Grand Union Canal in Regent's Park.

Americans are experts at the fast eat-out. They throw barbecue or camp stove, buns, 'burgers', trimmings from the freezer and chilled drinks into the car and are off – or they stop *en route* at one of the many fast food places and buy take-out, ready-cooked food that keeps warm in special polystyrene boxes until they reach their eating spot. Their casual attitude to eating out (never 'picnicking') means that more people can happily be scooped into an improvised feast. One of the happiest eat-outs I ever attended was in South Dakota, where at dusk in a natural amphitheatre among the arid stone hill fingers of the Badlands, trestle tables were set with cocktails and hamburgers sizzled on a barbecue. The beer was kept cold in chiller boxes and the hospitality was warm, getting warmer as the moon rose over our conviviality.

In Europe half the fun of eating out seems to be in the planning. A carrier bag can be kept in a kitchen cupboard, always ready with the basic essentials of salt, pepper, tube of mustard, plastic cutlery, paper plates, cups and bowls, napkins and a set of plastic drinking glasses, corkscrew (those fold-up ones are excellent) and tin opener.

STARTING FROM COLD

When school holidays approach and guests are expected with whom one plans a lot of sightseeing and days out the hostess with a deep freeze can plan her picnic menus and get them frozen well ahead. So on the day of the picnic she can just pile the foods into a bag. What's more they are ready chilled and can be packed round butter and cold drinks to keep them extra cold.

But some things don't freeze well. Never freeze hard-boiled eggs – they go rubbery – nor anything containing mayonnaise or salad cream. Take these dressings along separately. Nor do salad greens and tomatoes freeze well; they should not be used in sandwiches for the freezer.

Generally sandwiches do freeze well, though, and can be made weeks, even months, ahead. They should preferably have a creamy filling that will hold any meat, poultry or fish, and should be wrapped well in cling wrap or foil. Packed in polythene bags, they will thaw on the journey and be moist when needed.

Use softened butter and apply it generously to make sandwiches hold together. For extra flavour you can blend curry sauce, tomato purée, freshly chopped herbs or finely grated lemon rind with the butter.

Some fillings that are ideal for all types of picnic sandwich, but which freeze well include:

Quick pâté
Mix together roughly equal quantities of *pâté de foie* and cream cheese and season to taste with salt, pepper and garlic powder. (Remember, if freezing, that seasonings develop their flavour during freezing, so go steady, or take along seasonings for picnickers to add themselves.)

Sardine
Drain the oil from a can of sardines and mash them with a little tomato, pickle and grated onion.

Scrambled egg
Mix with crisply fried chopped bacon.

Cottage cheese
Mix with chutney and chopped ham.

Cream cheese
Mix with chopped walnuts and chopped dates (particularly good with brown bread).

9

Sweet sandwiches

Spread honey on brown bread and fill with thinly sliced bananas tossed in lemon juice to prevent them turning brown. Or mash bananas, grated chocolate and lemon juice and spread on brown bread.

Small sandwiches can be made and frozen as an *hors d'oeuvre* for more elegant picnic occasions. Remove the crusts from thin slices of bread, spread on butter and a creamy filling, roll them as tightly as possible, then wrap them in foil and freeze. The ends can be dipped in chopped parsley or chives for decoration.

Flans, among the most perfect of picnic foods, freeze extremely well. To save time in pastry-making, use mixes or the 'one-stage' method.

One-stage Flan Pastry

4oz/100g margarine or butter
6oz/175g plain flour
1 tablespoon water

Place margarine and 2 tablespoons of the flour with the water in a mixing bowl and cream with a fork for $\frac{1}{2}$ minute until well mixed. Stir in rest of flour. Knead on a lightly floured board until smooth. Roll out fairly thinly and line a 7in/18cm flan ring. Line with greaseproof paper and bake blind with baking beans at 400°F/200°C/Gas 6 for 15 minutes. Remove greaseproof paper, beans and flan ring and bake for a further 10–15 minutes.

The classic *quiche* Lorraine or an onion and cream flan are among my favourites for outdoor eating, but Summer Savoury Flan is quicker to make and gives a hint of both flavourings.

Summer Savoury Flan

1 flan case as above
4oz/100g cooked chopped ham
2oz/50g packet cream of onion or leek soup

$\frac{1}{2}$ pint/275ml water
3 eggs, beaten

Place chopped ham on partly cooked flan case. Mix packet
soup with water and beat in eggs. Pour over chopped ham
and bake at 375°F/190°C/Gas 5 for 30 minutes.
Garnish with tomatoes and parsley after freezing.

(Serves 4–6)

Two other delicious less-than-ordinary fillings are:

Bacon and Pineapple

8oz/225g can pineapple rings or slices, drained
4oz/100g streaky bacon, derinded, chopped and fried
2 eggs, beaten
$\frac{1}{4}$ pint/150ml milk
Seasoning

Arrange pineapple and bacon at bottom of flan case.
Beat eggs, milk and seasoning together and pour over.
Bake as above.   *(Serves 4)*

Crab and Asparagus

6oz/175g can crab meat, drained
15oz/425g can asparagus spears, drained; or use frozen
3 large eggs, beaten
$\frac{1}{2}$ pint milk
Seasoning

Arrange crab meat and asparagus in flan case. Beat eggs,
milk and seasoning together and pour over. Bake as above.

(Serves 4)

Pâtés, terrines and meat loaves also freeze well and as
well as the fast-to-make ones suggested below, more elaborate ones can be frozen, preferably in plastic or foil containers, ready for transportation. A strongly flavoured one
which goes well in the open air with French bread (also
freezable) and crisp salad vegetables is:

11

Herring Luncheon Terrine

4 herrings
Seasoning
2 hard-boiled eggs
1 cooking apple, grated
2oz/50g ground almonds
$\frac{1}{2}$ level teaspoon sugar

Clean and bone herrings. Lightly grill and skin fillets and
pound with a wooden spoon. Season, slice eggs and arrange
some slices on bottom of a greased $1\frac{1}{2}$ pint/750ml terrine
dish. Chop remaining slices, mix with pounded herrings
and other ingredients, and spoon into the terrine. Cover with
foil or lid and stand dish in a tin of water. Bake at
350°F/180°C/Gas 4 for 40 minutes.   (*Serves 4–6*)

Another sustaining terrine is made from a mixture of
sausages and chicken livers; or beef sausages can be used
instead of pork and calves' or lambs' liver instead of chicken.

Sausage and Chicken Terrine

1lb/500g pork sausages or sausagemeat
$\frac{1}{2}$lb/250g chopped chicken livers
1 clove garlic, crushed
Seasoning
1 teaspoon mixed herbs
1 onion, finely chopped
6 rashers streaky bacon
2 eggs
2 tablespoons sherry
10 stuffed olives
1 canned red pimento
Coloured aspic jelly (optional)

Skin the sausages. Mix with the chicken livers, garlic,
seasoning, herbs, onion, 4 of the bacon rashers (chopped),
eggs and sherry. Put half the mixture into an earthenware
terrine. Halve the olives and cut the pimento into strips.

Arrange over the bottom layer of the terrine. Top with the remaining terrine mixture and press well down. Lay the two remaining bacon rashers over the top. Cover with a piece of greased greaseproof paper and then with the lid. Stand in a roasting tin and add sufficient hot water to come halfway up the sides of the terrine.

Cook at 325°F/160°C/Gas 3 for 1½ hours. Remove from the tin of water and weight the top of the terrine. Leave until quite cold. For decoration, the top of the terrine can be layered with extra pimento and olive, and glazed with liquid aspic.

To freeze allow the terrine to become quite cold, then overwrap in foil or cling wrap. It can be frozen for up to 6 months. Thaw at room temperature for 4–6 hours before serving.   (*Serves 8*)

Cheeses can be frozen for about 3–4 months and small, individual portions of a selection, closely wrapped in foil and in an outer polythene wrapper or plastic box, can be assembled to mate, with fresh fruit and biscuits, an instant end to a picnic meal. As cheese is rather drying on the palate, grapes or juicy fruit should be available with it. An 8oz/250g piece of firm cheese will take 3–4 hours to thaw at room temperature.

ON YOUR MARKS, GET SET

Non freezer owners can also get off to an unexhausted start. If really pressed for time, the best idea is to pile basic ingredients for a sandwich bar into a large basket, remembering knives for spreading. Set them up on a board slung across the boot of the car or along a suitable flat log or wall top, and let everyone make up their own sandwiches.

It's as well to have an instant *hors d'oeuvre* ready to satisfy hungers while the sandwich bar is set up. Take a tray with the following on it covered with cling wrap.

3 large tomatoes, skinned and thinly sliced
2 hard-boiled eggs cut in half

8 slices German sausage
6 pickled gherkins
Grated carrot
2 pickled herrings, drained and cut in 1 in/25mm pieces
Pickled red cabbage
Watercress.   (*Serves 4*)

A quickly made pâté with French bread can also be used as a picnic starter.

Seafood Pâté

4oz/100g prawns
2oz/50g butter
Chopped parsley
Lemon juice
Seasoning

Pound prawns into a pulp. Mix with the butter, adding parsley and lemon juice to taste, plus seasoning. Chill in a plastic carrying box.   (*Serves 2–3*)

Kippers, preferably the ready-filleted type, make another quick starter, or can be used as a sandwich filling.

Kipper Pâté

4oz/100g kipper fillets
4oz/100g butter, softened
1 tablespoon lemon juice
Finely grated rind of $\frac{1}{2}$ a lemon
2 tablespoons white breadcrumbs
Pepper

Lightly boil the kipper fillets, flake and beat with the softened butter, lemon juice, lemon rind, breadcrumbs and pepper. If an electric blender is available, raw kipper fillets can be used. Lightly cooked fillets are easier to mix by hand.

14

If making sandwiches with this mixture spread bread with parsley butter made by beating 1 tablespoon chopped parsley and 1 tablespoon lemon juice into 4oz/100g softened butter.

Whole loaves flavoured into family-sized sandwiches with quickly made spreads, and open sandwiches, are other useful ideas. Cutting a loaf in three slices horizontally, filling with store cupboard or left-over ingredients, spiking together with thin skewers or cocktail sticks, and slicing through at the picnic site is a speedy send off:

Bumper Picnic Loaf with Savoury Butter

1 large loaf (round granary or large French loaves are
    suitable)
3oz/75g butter
1 tablespoon French mustard
1 tablespoon chopped parsley
Assorted cooked meats and sausages
Lettuce
3 tomatoes, sliced
$\frac{1}{2}$ cucumber, sliced
6 spring onions
4–6 slices strong cheese, cut into thin strips

Cut the loaf into three horizontally and scoop out some of the bread from the bottom crust. Cream together the butter, mustard and parsley. Spread the bread with this savoury butter and then build a giant sandwich using all the rest of the ingredients. Wrap firmly in foil or cling wrap.

A variation of the French piperade also uses a wide split loaf.

Picnic Piperade

French loaf
1 large onion, sliced
1 large green pepper, deseeded and sliced
1 garlic clove, crushed (optional)

½lb/500g tomatoes, skinned, deseeded and chopped
Oil for cooking
6 eggs, lightly beaten with
1 tablespoon water

Split loaf horizontally and remove some of the dough. Cook the onion, pepper and garlic in the oil in a frying pan for about 10 minutes until soft. Add the tomatoes and cook, stirring, for a further 3–5 minutes. Pour in the eggs and scramble them with the vegetables. Season to taste. As soon as the eggs are set, spoon the piperade into the loaf. Put top on. Press well together, wrap tightly in foil and chill until needed. Cut in thick slices on the picnic.

A selection of spreads, ready mixed and taken along in plastic containers with rolls, crispbreads, biscuits and sliced loaves again lets the picnickers do their own make-up thing. Using spreads avoids the need to take along separate butter, which invariably melts over everything else. Spread-yourself suggestions:

Lamburger
Mix 8oz/250g cooked minced lamb, 4oz/100g each of grated celery and cucumber, 2 tablespoons each mayonnaise and chilli sauce, 4oz/100g grated cheese, salt and pepper.

Creamed cheese
Mix 4oz/100g grated Cheddar cheese, 5 fl oz/142ml carton soured cream, salt, pepper, ½ bunch watercress or 4 chopped gherkins and 6 chopped, stuffed green olives. (This also goes well as a dunk for cold sausages.)

Tuna and Cucumber
Blend 7oz/198g can tuna (or pink salmon) with 3 tablespoons thick mayonnaise, 1 tablespoon chopped chives, 3in/8cm cucumber (finely chopped), salt and pepper.

Liptauer cheese spread
(Enough for 8 slices of bread.) Beat together 4oz/100g cream cheese, and 2oz/50g soft margarine until smooth, add

a little mustard, 3 chopped anchovy fillets and 3 chopped gherkins. Season well and stir in a little paprika.

Apricot cheese filling
Blend until smooth 9 canned apricot halves, well drained and mashed, $\frac{1}{4}$ cup processed cheese, $\frac{1}{4}$ teaspoon sugar, 1 tablespoon chopped nuts, $\frac{1}{4}$ teaspoon cinnamon.

Open sandwiches get quicker to assemble with practice. They need not be the perfect art form they are in Denmark, but they are not easy to carry without spoiling. The best solution is packing individual ones in separate boxes; or arrange on a tray, loosely cover with foil or cling wrap and place carefully in some part of the car where they will not be sat upon or damaged. For teenagers, massive open sandwiches called Pontoons are simple to make and filling. Split French loaves lengthways and butter each half. Cover each half with scrambled egg, pâté, sliced tomatoes, cream cheese and sliced luncheon meat. Place mustard and cress between each ingredient and the next.

Simple open sandwiches can be made using fairly thick slices of bread or crispbread. Their origin is said to be from the days when poor Scandinavians had no plates, and used bread slabs instead to place their food on. Butter each slice thickly to hold the toppings on, for example:

Wafer thin roast beef with mustard
Slice of ham, scrambled eggs and parsley sprigs
Slice of ham, green pepper ring filled with cream cheese
    and garnished with tomato wedges
Slices of luncheon meat topped with a spoonful of cottage
    cheese and garnished with mandarin orange segments
A lettuce leaf topped with cold chicken mixed with chutney
Cream cheese mixed with chopped prawns and chopped
    cucumber. Spread on thickly and garnish with whole
    prawns or parsley
Smoked haddock blended with softened butter, spread on
    and garnish with watercress
Sliced cucumber, cooked ham slices and sliced Edam

cheese with a topping of 1 tablespoon mayonnaise mixed
with 1 teaspoon mustard
Cream cheese and pepper, sliced radishes and chopped
spring onions (the Belgian worker's 'tartine' lunch)

Just as cold scrambled egg makes a nourishing, moist and
adaptable filling for sandwiches and helps hold open sandwiches together, cold omelettes and pancakes can also become quick, breadless picnic fare. I think hotels have a mean
idea of a packed lunch though one British chain now offers
'Happy Traveller' packs of cooked meat or pie, Scotch egg,
fresh fruit, rolls, butter, fruit cake, pie or yogurt plus drinks
to choice, which seems basically sensible. But most hotels
give you stale, butterless bread with a slab of gristle-bound
meat, hard-boiled eggs like bullets, an orange, curled
cheese and a wave of the hand. The best hotel picnic I ever
had was in the Azores, where the doorman handed into my
touring car a wicker basket of Edwardian proportions for
my lunch. I sat on the hydrangea-filled lip of one of the
island's many volcano craters and ate and ate. Apart from
the glory of thick damask napkins embroidered with the
hotel monogram and heavy silver plate cutlery, crystal wine
glasses with two carefully chosen half bottles, proper cruets
including English mustard to go with the fine rare beef, the
centrepiece was a cold omelette. It sounds a let down, but it
is an easily eaten and digested meal on the move.

When making omelettes for picnics, make them firmer
than usual, and flat – use 4–5 eggs in a 8in/20cm pan. Turn
to brown on both sides. Add chopped onion and sliced
mushrooms or asparagus tips to the mixture; diced cooked
potato and sliced green olives is another good combination.
Potatoes always help to keep the omelette moist. A big
cake-like omelette can be made with a similar filling and
carried cut in wedges to serve with a salad.

Holiday Open Omelette

Oil for frying
1 large onion, sliced,
1lb/456g can potatoes, cubed

4oz / 100g cheese, cubed
6 eggs, lightly beaten with
1 tablespoon water

Heat 2–3 tablespoons oil in a large frying pan. Add the onion and cook gently until soft. Add the potatoes and cook until both are golden. Stir in the cubes of cheese. Pour over the beaten eggs and stir round to make an open omelette. When just set, cut into wedges and serve with a salad.

(Serves 3–4)

Another idyllic picnic I remember was in northern Sweden on a lake shore backed with snow-capped mountains in early June. After canoeing we pulled into a small beach where our host had a fire blazing and coffee pot steaming away. As we warmed ourselves around the fire and quenched inner fires with the fire and ice of aquavit and chilled beer, sausage-shaped parcels in foil were handed round. These turned out to be a thin pancake spread with a sweetish, creamed goat's milk cheese. Thin pancakes, which can be made in advance and frozen, also make a good dessert, filled with plum jam and whipped cream, rolled up and carefully sealed in foil.

Though fresh fruit is always an ideal end to an informal picnic, desserts do not have to take long to make and on the whole are not the most important part of a picnic meal. Yogurt can be used as the base for simple fruit mixes. Or make a yogurt whip by beating an egg yolk with a tablespoon of sugar and a few drops of vanilla essence until thick and pale. Fold into a 6oz / 170g carton of yogurt. Whisk egg white and fold in. Serve yogurt mixed with fresh raspberries, strawberries and blackberries – gooseberries are especially good – or any tinned fruit. Use yogurt cartons for carrying individual desserts and seal with foil and rubber bands.

Use canned custard or rice pudding to cut take-off time. Slice two peeled bananas and two oranges, fold into canned custard and carry in an airtight polythene container. Top with chopped nuts. In small cartons, layer drained, canned mandarin oranges with canned rice pudding.

3
Well Beached

The seaside ideal seems to be transatlantic – big sandy strands backed by dunes, like Marconi beach on Cape Cod, and either bright sun and surf or dusk with a driftwood fire, seafood grilling, a guitar being played, chilled beer and finally hot coffee laced with brandy or rum as the embers settle to the sand.

Certainly the reality often includes sand – in everything from eyes to wine glasses, not to mention tar on the table-cloth, wind-blown smoke from a fire that has taken hours to encourage into life. If the fish pâté wasn't smoked before, it soon will be – and insects have to be repelled with a spray as they dive-bomb the food.

Best to take a wind-break and a small camping Gaz single-burner stove or a small barbecue for beach cookery. There'll be plenty of water near by to put out any fire that gets out of hand; a bucket rather larger than the child's variety is useful and can help keep the wine cool. A metal bucket can double as a container for seafood, collected or bought, which can then be cooked over the fire in it in sea water (no need to remember the salt this time). Alternatively, upturned it becomes a cook's fire-tending seat. An upturned box or small table helps to keep food and drink out of the sand.

A beach picnic needn't be beside the sea. Rivers and lakes have attractive beaches, often of soft clean sand, that make tranquil settings. I have sweet memories of such places. Beside New Chum falls in the Blyde ('joyful') river canyon of South Africa. The smoothed grey rocks, big as London buses across the rapids, become small and squared beside the dammed-up water pools to make a natural fireplace for a camp-fire stew of corned beef, baked beans, herbs, slosh of red wine and canned vegetables. The midnight sun of a mid-summer's eve in north Norway, taking photos of our fresh fish cooking over a lake-side fire, eaten boiled plainly with salt, melted butter and thin crisp bread and, of course, washed down with cold beer. Then there were several Canadian sunsets alongside rushing rivers in the north-west; taking a camping truck off the main road, down a track, into a clearing, Scotch was taken literally on the river rocks while planning a chowder and chops supper as the ever plentiful wood prickled into flame.

The worst of cooking on an open fire is the black carbon that forms on the cooking utensils and that no known detergent seems to shift. I don't know what the solution is – perhaps keeping an old pot solely for picnicking or covering base and rim with foil each time.

An alternative is to cook food in the embers of an open fire, wrapped in foil that can be discarded afterwards. This is fun but it takes ages and sea-air-whetted appetites can turn to sharp tongues before the food is even half edible. One way to enjoy the primitive 'me Tarzan, you Jane' open-air fire cookery is to part-cook items at home, then reheat and finish them in the embers when the fire is right. With a beach fire it's a good idea to pile up stones as a base and get them red hot before putting in the food. In a big fire the places where the food is ember-covered should be marked with stones so the food isn't lost. Retrieve it with tongs (the longer handled the better) or a meat fork. Take similar utensils along to barbecues (see Chapter 8), also a pair of oven gloves. And take lots of foil – to eat off, to wrap things in and to contain hot foods.

Jacket-baked potatoes take long enough to cook at home, even when speeded by piercing with a skewer. So pre-cook and wrap them in foil (they can even be frozen in advance), then reheat them in the embers for about 40 minutes and serve with grilled sausages and lots of melted butter or chopped chives and sour cream sauce.

Frozen vegetables placed in foil with seasoning, butter and 4 tablespoons of water can be cooked at the edge of the fire for 25 minutes. Frozen mixed vegetables, frozen peas, frozen sweetcorn are all excellent this way.

Chicken portions can also be pre-cooked, seasoned and heated through in foil. More flavour can be added if butter and chopped onion are cooked in the foil with them. Chicken joints, cooked from scratch in foil in the centre of the fire, will take 45–50 minutes. Lamb cutlets also make fine hot finger foods for beach picnics. At home brush the cutlets with mint jelly, and season, then fry in oil or grill until cooked through. When cold, coat them with sausagemeat, dip in beaten egg, coat with breadcrumbs and wrap in double foil, to be reheated in hot embers for 15 minutes.

Even a dessert can be cooked in the fire. For Banana Marshmallow place 2 peeled bananas on a piece of foil, put two marshmallows on each banana and dot with butter, fold over foil ends to make a loose parcel, sealing edges well, and cook at the edge of a fire for 10 minutes. I'm delicious, fry me!

For camp fire enthusiasts who want to fry their own picnic, eggs and bacon with chunks of bread are basic, but take non-stick pans and long-handled fish slices to make things easier. More adventurous is bacon with thinly cut liver, and fried trout with bacon is tasty. The trout should be rolled in seasoned flour and fried in butter. French toast – bread slices dipped in beaten and seasoned egg and fried – makes a good raft for bacon or tomatoes. There's also a Danish dish called Burning Love which lives up to its reputation.

Burning Love

1lb / 500g potatoes
1oz / 25g butter
A little milk
Seasoning
½ lb / 250g streaky bacon, derinded and chopped
2 sliced onions
Pickled beetroot

Peel and boil potatoes. Mash with butter, milk and seasoning; keep hot. Fry bacon until crisp, then fry sliced onion in bacon fat. Arrange bacon on potatoes and surround with onion and diced cold pickled beetroot.

A sustaining fried dish, quick and easy to create, is Corned Beef Hash. Preferably pre-mix a tin of corned beef with diced or mashed potatoes (12oz / 350g meat to 1lb / 500g potatoes). Mix in finely chopped onion, seasoning and chopped parsley. At the picnic spread the mixture in a pan with hot fat and brown it gently for 10–15 minutes, turning frequently with a wide spatula. Serve in wedges.

BUCKET AND SPADE COOKERY

A joy of the old-fashioned seaside holiday was catching shrimps, mussels and crabs. Sea pollution has stopped much of this but it's still possible to catch your own lunch – or at least to buy it fresh from local fishermen.

Mussels, taken below the low-tide line in non-polluted areas, and winkles are good. Crabs are more difficult to find, though the children at Bude in Cornwall catch them with simple string, pin and limpet line in the old canal. The small red-backed variety are delicious when steamed.

Seafood *must* be fresh, and preparation and cooking on the beach fire must be done properly.

Prawns and Shrimps
If still alive, plunge into pan or metal bucket of boiling sea water after washing off excess salt. Cook for about 1

minute until they become pinkish, then drain. Throw out any damaged or discoloured ones. Eat with brown bread and lemon juice.

Crabs
These need to be killed before cooking or they shed claws. Push a skewer in just above the mouth to penetrate the spinal cord. Cook in a large pan or bucket of warm salted water – adding herbs and vinegar if available – bringing slowly to the boil. Cook for 15 minutes to the pound. Dressing the crab is fiddly under beach conditions but patience and a hammer help. Remove the small sac below the head, also the part known for its shape as dead man's fingers in the body. Scrape meat off with skewer or small metal spoon. With the hammer crack the main inner shell to the rim, leaving the outer shell for serving. When all the meat is out, mix brown meat with some fine breadcrumbs and season well, adding a little vinegar or lemon juice and preferably Tabasco or Worcestershire Sauce. Arrange the meat in the main shell with white meat around it.

Lobster
If you are lucky enough to afford a lobster and buy one live from the fisherman, kill it by plunging it into boiling salt water and cook for 10–15 minutes per pound. Remove the greenish sac and grey spongy gills from the head and the dark intestine running down the back. Crack the large claws with a stone or hammer.

Mussels
These are probably the easiest to get and cook on the beach. Discard any that are slightly open and use only tightly closed ones still alive at the time of cooking. Wash thoroughly several times before leaving covered with cold water for about 30 minutes to allow any sand to drop to the bottom. Scrub well to remove dirt, and trim off any remaining seaweed and whiskers.

Moules Marinière
This is a simple way of serving mussels. Put them in a pan

with some dry white wine (about 1 pint/500ml wine and 1 pint/500ml water to 6 pints/3litres mussels). As the mussels open add chopped parsley and some chopped onion or shallot. Garlic also may be added. Cover and bring slowly to boil. Boil for about 2 minutes and discard any mussels that still remain closed. Double cream ($\frac{1}{2}$ pint/250ml) can be added at the end of cooking, bringing the liquid back to the boil. Serve in soup plates, using empty mussel shells as spoons.

My most naturally primitive picnic, owing nothing to anything man-made, was on a beach near Freetown, in Sierra Leone. Black dug-out canoes came in over the reefs, bringing brightly coloured fish and a baby shark with skin like silk. A snapper was gutted and threaded on thin sticks cut from a palm frond while a boy gathered dry coconut fibre and rubbed sticks together until it lit. When the fish cooked, a boy climbed the palm for a coconut milk cocktail to be drunk, cool from the shell. Then the fish was served on a plantain leaf platter. Fingers sufficed to dig out the rich white flesh. Later a swim in the sea washed the grease away.

Fresh fish should be gutted by slitting with a sharp knife from under the head to halfway down the underside, then removing entrails and trimming tail and fins. Small fish can be grilled over a beach fire barbecue style with a sharpened stick or skewer through them. Mackerel, which is cheap – in certain places free, as fishermen often discard it – is a much underrated fish that needs no added fat. Plaice and sole should be rubbed with oil or butter before cooking.

All these fish can be wrapped in double thickness foil, with herbs and seasoning, and cooked in the embers or on a grid over the fire. Mackerel is traditionally accompanied with a gooseberry sauce. It is equally good served cold. Cold Orange Mackerel can be prepared in advance or grilled at the picnic.

Cold Orange Mackerel

3 medium-sized mackerel

Marinade
8 tablespoons oil
5 tablespoons white wine
Few drops Tabasco
Salt and freshly ground black pepper

Garnish
2oz/50g black olives
2 oranges, peeled and sliced into rings
Fresh bay leaves

Clean, gut and wash the mackerel and remove heads. Make two slanting incisions with a sharp knife across both sides of each fish. Lay the mackerel in the grill pan and pour over the mixed oil, wine and seasonings. Leave the fish in the marinade for two hours, turning occasionally. Place pan under preheated grill and cook the fish for 5–8 minutes on each side, depending on thickness. When cooked, lift the mackerel carefully on to a serving dish. Pour over juices from the pan and when fish is quite cold, garnish with olives, orange rings and bay leaves.   (*Serves 3*)

One of the most filling and flavoursome of soups is a chowder made from fish or seafood plus potatoes and cream. Scallops, clams and oysters, though expensive, are delicious cooked this way. This chowder using cider as its base can be made on a large scale in advance, carried in a large airtight plastic container and reheated in a metal container on the fire.

Seafood Chowder

1 medium-sized onion, finely sliced
2oz/50g butter
2½oz/70g flour
1½ pints/850ml cider
1 pint/575ml water
6½oz/180g can crab meat (drained)
3oz/85g can lobster meat (drained)
¼ pint/150ml shelled cockles

¼ pint/150ml shelled mussels
3oz/85g can shrimps (drained)
Grated rind of 1 lemon
Seasoning

Lightly fry onion in butter until tender but not brown. Stir
in flour and cook for a minute. Remove from heat and
gradually stir in cider and water. Return to heat and bring
to the boil, stirring. Add crab meat, lobster meat, cockles,
mussels, shrimps, lemon rind and seasoning. Cover and
simmer gently for 20 minutes.   (*Serves 8–10*)

DINING IN THE DUNES

On a hot day at the beach getting a tan is pleasanter than
rushing about collecting seafood or trying to find a fish-
seller. A well-planned hamper, with foods carefully wrapped
in foil to keep out sand, averts queueing at the cafés. Food
should be cool and easy to eat. Finger-licking-good is the
ideal, no messing about with knives and forks; the sea is
your finger bowl. Highly suitable are cold chicken drumsticks and other easily eaten meats, cold fish dishes and massive mixed pasta salads that one can eat from a bowl with a
spoon.

When everyone comes back from the first swim or ex-
ploring the beach a ready-to-eat *hors d'oeuvre* will sus-
tain them. Children will like to make up their own mini
kebabs from a big box containing tiny tomatoes, whole or
halved mushrooms, diced cucumber, radishes, cheese cubes,
chunks of celery, green pepper strips, shredded lettuce and
cold cooked sausage chunks. Provide cocktail sticks for
skewering the bits and a bowl of Mustard Dip for the kebabs
made by blending 4 tablespoons mayonnaise, 2 tablespoons
tomato ketchup, 1 teaspoon French mustard and 1 teaspoon
tarragon vinegar.

Cold sausages split lengthways and filled with curd cheese
mixed with horseradish sauce make another good starter.
An unusual starter is Onions in Cider.

27

Onions in Cider

1 litre bottle cider
2lb/1kg pickling sized onions
4oz/100g raisins
Dark brown sugar to taste

Reduce cider to a quarter of its volume. Cover onions with cold water and bring to the boil. Remove from the heat, skin onions and arrange in a buttered fireproof dish. Sprinkle raisins over the top. Add about two tablespoons of dark brown sugar to the cider, pour over and cook in the oven at 350°F/180°C/Gas 4 for 15 minutes. Serve very cold.

(Serves 4)

Herrings certainly smack of the sea and are beloved of the Dutch, who eat them in raw chunks from the street stalls as a morning stimulator. For beach picnics they are nutritious and can be served cold. This fish accepts different flavours easily. Herring Kaassla with bread makes a good picnic main course.

Herring Kaassla

6oz/175g Gouda cheese
1 apple
6 sticks celery
6 gherkins
6oz/175g cooked peas
Small packet frozen mixed vegetables, cooked
Seasoning
Mayonnaise
6 rollmop herrings
6oz/175g grapes
Parsley

Cut the cheese, apple, celery and gherkins into small cubes. Mix with peas, mixed vegetables and seasoning, Blend with a little mayonnaise and pile in a dish. Arrange rollmops over the top and garnish with halved depipped grapes and parsley.

Perhaps chicken is too easily assumed to be the meat that all men love when travelling and much airline food could be described as a chicken joke. But drumsticks prepared with flavour marinated into them approach the Henry VIII hearty eating image. (Don't, like bluff King Hal, toss the bones over the shoulder. Bones and any refuse should be taken home in plastic bags or placed in litter bins. Never bury it in the sand or shingle; out of sight is definitely not out of mind when children or animals scrape up a ragged sardine can or broken bottle.)

Marinated chicken legs
Place 4 tablespoons wine vinegar or lemon juice, 1 crushed garlic clove, a little chopped parsley and seasoning in a shallow dish. Put 4–8 chicken legs in this marinade and leave for at least 2 hours in a cool place. Turn them occasionally. Drain chicken and grill under medium heat for 10–15 minutes, brushing with the marinade until tender and golden brown. Serve with salad.

Drumsticks can also be cooked and served cold with a sauce as in Elizabethan Chicken.

Elizabethan Chicken

4 large or 8 small chicken drumsticks
1 sliced onion
Salt and pepper
2 level teaspoons gelatine
5 tablespoons hot water
Milk
2oz/50g butter
2oz/50g flour
6 tablespoons salad cream

Lay the drumsticks in a large saucepan, add the onion and
$\frac{1}{2}$ teaspoon salt and just cover with water. Cook until tender.
Drain off the stock, remove the skin from the drumsticks
and allow to cool. Dissolve the gelatine in the water. Make
the stock up to $\frac{1}{2}$ pint/275ml with milk and make a thick

white sauce with the butter, flour and liquor. Fold the salad cream into the sauce and adjust seasoning. Stir in the dissolved gelatine. Coat the drumsticks with the sauce. If it becomes too thick, warm over a low heat. Cool on wire rack and wrap carefully in foil or cling wrap.   (*Serves 4*)

Cold Spicy Chicken

4 chicken joints
¼ pint/150ml chicken stock (or stock cube)
1 teaspoon turmeric
1 teaspoon curry powder
1 teaspoon ground ginger
1 teaspoon mustard
½ teaspoon ground pepper
½ teaspoon mixed herbs
¼ teaspoon mixed spice
1oz/25g butter
Mango chutney

Poach the joints in stock until tender. Mix together the herbs and spices and sprinkle this over the drained and dried joints of chicken. Leave for half an hour. Then brush with melted butter and put under the grill until they turn golden brown and crisp. Leave to cool. Serve with mango chutney.
(*Serves 4*)

Corned beef can be served cold in a tomato-flavoured jelly. Small portions can be set in individual containers for a starter or larger amounts for a main course.

Corned Beef in Aspic

2 packets powdered aspic (enough for 1 pint/575ml)
¾ pint/425ml hot water
¼ pint/150ml tomato juice
1 hard-boiled egg, sliced
7oz/198g can corned beef, chilled and diced
Small packet frozen mixed vegetables, cooked, drained
    and cooled

Dissolve aspic in the hot water. Stir in tomato juice and allow to cool slightly. Place 1 tablespoon aspic in six individual cartons or plastic cups and place in a refrigerator until set. Place a slice of hard-boiled egg on the set aspic, then add enough liquid aspic just to cover the egg. Return to the refrigerator until set. Repeat with diced corned beef and mixed vegetables until all the ingredients are used, allowing aspic to set between each layer.   (*Serves 6*)

The easiest way of taking meat to the beach is to encase it in pastry which can be sliced through easily.

Picnic Slice

2oz/50g onion, chopped
1oz/25g fat for frying
2 tablespoons tomato ketchup
Seasoning
8oz/225g pork sausagemeat
3oz/75g cooking fat
8oz/225g self-raising flour
¼ teaspoon mixed herbs
6–7 tablespoons water

Fry the onion in fat until tender. Add the tomato ketchup, seasoning and onion to sausagemeat; mix well. Rub fat into flour, add a pinch of salt and the herbs. Bind with water and mix until the pastry leaves the sides of the bowl. Roll out on a floured board to a rectangle 9 × 11in/23 × 28cm. Spread with sausage mixture and roll up lightly, starting from a long side. Place on a well-greased baking sheet. Make cuts along top at intervals. Brush with milk or beaten egg. Bake at 375°F/190°C/Gas 5 for 20 minutes; reduce to 350°F/180°C/Gas 4 for another 20 minutes.   (*Serves 4–6*)

Beach picnics should certainly be salad days; but the salads should not be thin, jaded and slithery; they should be cut fine but have body, and combined with some kind of sauce or mayonnaise to make them easily edible from bowls or plastic containers with fork or spoon. Pasta Slaw is inexpensive and substantial.

Pasta Slaw

3oz/75g spaghetti rings
  or any short-cut pasta
3oz/75g white cabbage
½ small green pepper
1 small carrot
1 tablespoon chopped chives
Scant ¼ pint/150ml mayonnaise
1 tablespoon soured cream
1 tablespoon vinegar
2 teaspoons sugar

Cook the spaghetti rings. When just tender ('al dente') drain
and refresh with cold water. Prepare the vegetables: finely
shred the cabbage, deseed and dice the green pepper and
grate the carrot. Add the chives and pack into a plastic
container with the pasta. Mix soured cream, vinegar and
sugar. Carry in a separate jar to picnic. Mix well with
vegetables before serving.   (*Serves 4*)

Midsummer Salad

1lb/500g pork sausages
½oz/15g fat for frying
2oz/50g walnut halves
8oz/225g carton cottage cheese
15oz/428g can pineapple segments, drained
Seasoning
Lettuce

Fry the sausages gently for about 20 minutes until cooked
and browned. Drain and allow to become cold. Chop the
walnuts and cut the cold sausages into slices. Add the nuts,
sausages and the pineapple to the cheese, add a little
seasoning and mix lightly. At the picnic, serve with lettuce.
                                                (*Serves 4*)

The following is an unusual mixture of strawberries and
ham which helps minimise thirst.

Strawberry Fare

1 grapefruit, peeled and sliced
1 green pepper, deseeded and sliced
4oz/100g cubed ham
2oz/50g sliced mushrooms
2 sliced apples
4oz/100g washed, halved strawberries
Seasoning
Juice of ½ lemon
1 cos lettuce, washed

Mix together grapefruit, green pepper, ham, mushrooms,
apples and strawberries. Season to taste and stir in lemon
juice. Carry lettuce separately and serve as base for the
fruit and meat mixture.   (*Serves 4*)

4
Winter Trails

The Norwegians enjoy meals eaten out in crisp, cold weather. At weekends, families don cross-country skis and strap on packs containing simple food which they eat trekking through the silent snow-bound forests and over thick lake ice. Certainly they have no problem about chilling their cans of beer.

In Britain a New Year's day party I gave in the country became an *al fresco* feast, with guests taking their food into the crisp sunlight of the garden. Conversely a mid-summer patio party turned into a miserable crouch round the fire on a drizzly grey evening. So it's a case of 'grab the grub and get going' on cold but clear days. There's no better after-the-turkey-and-plum-pud-satiation than a Boxing Day picnic in the country at the end of a long walk. Cold turkey left-overs are as good outdoors as at the dining table; cold fried plum pudding with a liberal spreading of brandy or rum butter tastes a thousand times better in the open air than even on Christmas Day.

Food for a winter picnic should have a spark of warmth in itself if none of the 'hot meals in a mug' in Chapter 7 is taken along. Ginger, cinnamon, cloves or curry powder can be added to give dishes an inner glow. Drinks in a flask could be mulled ale or cider or the simplest of hot wine cups (see Chapter 10), and if a drive is involved black coffee can be taken, laced with miniatures of Scotch, brandy or rum for the non-drivers. Queen Victoria, that keen picnicker around Balmoral, was not averse to Highland tea, a delicate, lady-like brew strengthened against Scotch mists with a drop of the local malt.

Above all the food should be easy to eat with one hand. Damp and cold may not always allow a sit-down meal and using a knife and fork while perched on log, gate or wall top is virtually impossible. Cold day picnickers may be reluctant to take off their gloves for long periods; foil-wrapped food that can be eaten in one gloved hand is of the essence.

Sandwiches, cold and moist for a summer day, appear just soggy on a cold day. Better than bread are flavoured and filled loaves that can be eaten in slab-like slices.

Cheese Loaf

3oz/75g margarine
8oz/225g self-raising flour
1 level teaspoon baking powder } sieved
1 level teaspoon dry mustard } together
½ level teaspoon salt
¼ level teaspoon pepper
4 rashers bacon, derinded and chopped
1 egg
3oz/75g Cheddar cheese, grated
¼ pint/150ml milk

Sieve all the dry ingredients in a mixing bowl, add the remainder and beat together with a wooden spoon until well mixed (2–3 minutes). Place the mixture in a deep 1lb/500g loaf tin, previously bottom-lined with greaseproof paper and brushed with melted margarine. Smooth over the top. Bake on the middle shelf of a preheated moderate oven (375°F/190°C/Gas 5) for 40–45 minutes. Remove from the oven and leave in the tin for 5 minutes before turning out. When cold, slice and spread with margarine or butter.

Pastry is an excellent wrapping material for foods and crisp and light for a winter day. Cornish miners' wives long ago discovered pastry as the basis of the perfect portable meal to be eaten in cramped conditions. The pasty was pocket shaped and the pastry enclosed any scraps of mixed meat or vegetables they could find for the miners' pit meal. Critics said the pastry was so hard that if a pasty was dropped down a mine shaft, it would survive intact. And the Devil would never cross the Tamar river boundary into Cornwall for fear of being made into a pasty.

Almost anything can be enclosed in a pasty: leftover meat, vegetables, bacon and egg, apple or fish.

Egg and Sardine Envelope

2 × 7oz/198g cans sardines in olive oil
4 eggs, hard-boiled and chopped
1 level tablespoon chopped parsley
2 level tablespoons tomato purée
Salt and pepper
10oz/275g shortcrust pastry
1 egg, beaten

Drain sardines, discard bones and flake fish. Add eggs, parsley, tomato purée and seasoning, mix well. Prepare the shortcrust pastry and roll out to a 12in/30cm square. Place on a baking tray. Shape filling to a 7in/18cm square in the centre of the pastry, and brush edges of pastry with water. Draw corners of pastry up to meet in the middle, and to enclose filling. Press edges together firmly. Brush with beaten egg and bake in a moderately hot oven
(400°F/200°C/Gas 6) for 25–30 minutes until golden brown and filling is heated through.   (*Serves 4–5*)

Sausage, Apple and Raisin Pasties

8 sausages
½oz/15g bacon fat or butter
12oz/350g cooking or dessert apples
2–3 dessertspoons raisins or sultanas
Juice of ½ a lemon
Ground cinnamon or nutmeg to taste
1 egg, beaten
12oz/350g shortcrust pastry

Skin the sausages and fry in the hot fat until golden all
over, then leave to cool. Peel, core and chop the apples,
mix with the dried fruit, sprinkle generously with lemon
juice and sparingly with the ground spice, then mix well.
Add sufficient beaten egg to bind. Roll out the pastry about
¼in/6mm thick and cut 8 circles about 6in/15cm diameter.
   Divide the apple filling between the circles, piling it in a
semi-circle on one half of each one. Place a sausage on top.
Brush the edges of the pastry with egg and fold over in a
half-moon shape. Press the pastry edges firmly together
and crimp by squeezing between finger and thumb into
little scallops. Add a spoonful of water to the remaining egg
and brush all over the pasties. Place them on a greased
baking tray. Make a couple of little slits in each pasty for
the steam to escape. Bake in a preheated moderately
hot oven (400°F/200°C/Gas 6) until well risen and golden
brown.   (*Makes 8*)

Ratatouille Pasties

2oz/50g butter
8oz/225g courgettes, wiped and sliced
1 medium aubergine, wiped and chopped
4oz/100g onion, skinned and chopped
8oz/225g tomatoes, skinned and roughly sliced
1 clove garlic, skinned and crushed
Freshly milled black pepper
2oz/57g can anchovies, drained and chopped
1lb/450g shortcrust pastry
1 egg, beaten

Melt the butter and fry courgettes, aubergine and onion together for 5 minutes. Stir in tomatoes and garlic, season with pepper and cook rapidly until no free liquid remains. Stir in anchovies. Cool. Divide pastry into 6 and roll out each piece to a large circle. Divide ratatouille mixture between pastry circles. Brush edges with egg and seal into pasty shapes. Brush with beaten egg and bake at 400°F/200°C/Gas 6 for about 25 minutes. Cool on a wire rack.

(Makes 6)

Savoury Turnovers

2 hard-boiled eggs, chopped; or 3oz/75g cooked minced
    meat or flaked smoked haddock
¼ pint/150ml cheese sauce
Salt and pepper
8oz/225g shortcrust pastry
6 teaspoons tomato chutney

Mix meat, egg or fish with cheese sauce and season. Roll out pastry thinly and cut into 6in/15cm rounds. Moisten edges of pastry and spread 1 teaspoon chutney over centre of each round. Put a heaped tablespoon of the filling on top. Fold pastry in half, seal and press edges together well. Bake for 20 minutes in a preheated oven at 400°F/200°C/Gas 6.

(Makes 6)

A deep-fried version of a pasty is Samosas.

Samosas

1 small onion, minced
1 teaspoon curry powder
Oil for frying
6oz/175g finely diced cooked lamb
Salt and pepper
1 tablespoon chutney
8oz/225g suet pastry

Fry onion and curry powder in a little oil for about 3–5 minutes. Add lamb and cook for another five minutes. Add

seasoning and chutney. Mix well and allow to cool
completely. Make up suet pastry, and roll out and cut into
6–8 rounds. Place a small amount of cooled mixture in
centre of pastry and bring up dampened edges to seal into
a pasty shape. Deep-fry pasties in hot oil for about 5–10
minutes until pastry is cooked.   (*Makes 6–8*)

Pastry can also be used in other ways to make winter
picnic fare. It can enclose burgers, form a giant sausage roll
or make a savoury egg roll which is slightly quicker to pro-
duce than individual pasties and can be taken along whole
and sliced as required.

Burger Puff

13oz/368g packet frozen puff pastry
4 beefburgers
2 tomatoes, sliced
1 onion, cut into rings
Seasoning
Pinch mixed herbs
Egg for glazing

Roll out pastry into an oblong about ¼in/6mm thick, large
enough to take 8 burgers. Cut in half and place one half on
a baking sheet. Place the burgers on top, leaving ½in/12mm
border around the edge. Top each of the burgers with
tomatoes, onion, seasoning and herbs. Roll out the
remaining half of pastry a little more. Sprinkle with flour
and fold in half lengthwise. Cut slits in the folded edge at
½in/12mm intervals, to within 1in/25mm of the open edges.
Brush edges with egg, place folded pastry on top half of the
burgers and unfold. Trim and seal edges. Brush with egg
and bake at 425°F/220°C/Gas 7 for 35–40 minutes.
                                                   (*Serves 4*)

Giant Sausage Roll

8oz/225g shortcrust pastry
1lb/500g pork sausagemeat

4 hard-boiled eggs
Egg or milk to glaze

Make up pastry as usual and roll thinly into an oblong about 11 × 9in/28 × 23cm. Flatten sausagemeat on a floured board to about 11 × 4in/28 × 10cm. Place on pastry. Place eggs along centre in line and lift sausagemeat to cover eggs. Brush the pastry edge with water and fold over sausage. Seal. Make a diagonal cut over each egg and glaze with beaten egg or milk. Bake in preheated moderately hot oven (400°F/200°C/Gas 6) for 30 minutes, then reduce to 380°F/190°C/Gas 5 for a further 30 minutes. Cool on a wire rack.

NOTE: Finely chopped onions, fried with 2 chopped bacon rashers and mixed into the sausagemeat, can be substituted for the eggs.   (*Serves 6–8*)

Savoury Egg Roll

8oz/225g shortcrust pastry
2oz/50g ham, chopped
3 hard-boiled eggs
¼ pint/150ml white sauce
Seasoning

Roll out the pastry into a square ⅛in/3mm thick. Mix together the ham, chopped hard-boiled eggs, sauce and seasoning, and spread over the pastry. Damp the edges and roll up as for jam roll. Bake in a moderately hot oven (400°F/200°C/Gas 6) for 20 minutes. Allow to cool. To serve cut the roll across in slices.   (*Serves 4*)

NOTE: This recipe could also be made with cheese-flavoured pastry for extra taste.

REMEMBER, REMEMBER...

One of Britain's most cherished festivals is Bonfire Night, on 5th November, and many people accompany the firework-watching and the burning of the Guy with an outdoor meal. Mugs of hot soup keep small children warm, and jacket-baked potatoes are popular whether cooked indoors or in the embers of the bonfire. For such a picnic not too far from home piping hot jacket-baked potatoes, well wrapped in foil, can be bundled in a teatowel which will keep them hot for about half an hour. They also act as wonderful hand warmers and are not too bad eaten cold.

Potato Splits

4 large potatoes, scrubbed and dried
2oz/50g butter
6oz/175g Edam cheese, thinly sliced
2oz/50g salami, sliced

Prick the skins of the potatoes with a fork and bake in a moderately hot oven (400°F/200°C/Gas 6) until they feel soft when pinched – about 1–1½ hours. Split the cooked potatoes 3 times lengthwise and insert a small knob of butter with slices of cheese and salami in each split. Wrap in foil and reheat for about 5 minutes. Wrap the foil-covered potatoes in a teatowel to keep warm for the picnic. (*Serves 4*)

Cheese Straws

6oz/175g plain flour
1 rounded teaspoon mustard powder
Salt and paprika pepper
3oz/75g butter
3oz/75g grated Cheddar cheese
1 large egg yolk
Egg or milk to glaze

Sift the flour and mustard with a pinch of salt and a dash of paprika pepper into a mixing bowl. Grate the butter, straight from the refrigerator into the bowl and rub in lightly. Stir in the cheese. Beat the egg yolk with 2 tablespoons cold water and use to bind the mixture – if necessary add a little more water so that the dough is firm but manageable. Knead lightly on a floured board and roll out into a rectangle.

Cut lengthways into about a dozen strips approximately ½in/12mm wide. Place these strips on a lightly greased baking tray, twisting them over. Brush over with beaten egg or milk and bake at 400°F/200°C/Gas 6 for 10–15 minutes. Remove very carefully from the baking sheet and cool on a wire rack. Can be served with a dip.

Honeyed Toffee Apples

8 small red eating apples
8 wooden meat skewers
5 tablespoons clear honey
8oz/225g demerara sugar
1oz/25g butter
1 tablespoon Golden Syrup
5 tablespoons water
2 teaspoons vinegar or lemon juice

Wash and dry the apples and press a stick into the stalk end of each. Heat the honey in a small pan over low heat until dissolved. Put the remaining ingredients into a thick-bottomed saucepan and stir over low heat until all the sugar has dissolved. Bring to the boil, stirring occasionally, and then boil steadily for 10–12 minutes without stirring. Drop a teaspoonful of the mixture into cold water in a saucer; it should set instantly and crack all over if broken. (A sugar thermometer should reach 290°F/145°C.) Allow the bubbles to die down, then dip the apples first into the honey and then into the toffee, tilting the pan so the apples are well coated. Place the apples on greased greaseproof paper until set – about 30–40 minutes. Wrap separately in plastic food wrap or waxed paper and store in an airtight tin.

Winter salads are not as cooling as they sound, given a sound heart of sausage, potato or pasta, and perhaps a touch of curry powder. The simplest is a mixture of grated apple, carrot and shredded white cabbage, with a dressing made of beaten eggs, soured cream and vinegar. The Germans go for hearty combinations that can be carried in sealed containers and eaten with a spoon.

Bavarian Cabbage Salad

1 medium white cabbage
4 tablespoons vegetable oil
Salt
Caraway seed
1 small onion, finely chopped
4oz/100g diced streaky bacon
3 tablespoons wine vinegar
Sugar

Quarter cabbage, remove stalk and shred. Heat 1 tablespoon vegetable oil and a little salted water containing a pinch of caraway seed. Put in shredded cabbage, cover with tight-fitting lid and cook for about 5 minutes; drain. Fry the chopped onion and diced bacon until golden brown. Add to the cabbage. Make dressing from remaining vegetable oil, wine vinegar, sugar and salt to taste; add to the cabbage mixture   (*Serves 4*)

Cauliflower Yogurt Salad

1 medium-sized cauliflower
Salt and pepper
1 green pepper
1 red pepper
2 stalks celery
4oz/100g button mushrooms

Dressing
5oz/142g carton natural yogurt

1 dessertspoon tomato ketchup
2 teaspoons lemon juice

Break off the cauliflower florets and wash them. Have a
pan of salted boiling water ready and drop them in. Bring
them back to the boil for 2 minutes, drain and rinse in cold
water. (They can be used raw if preferred.) Cut the peppers
in half, remove the core and seeds; shred the flesh quite
finely. Cut the celery into $\frac{1}{2}$in/12mm pieces. Wash, dry and
slice the mushrooms crossways. Mix all the vegetables
together and place in a bowl. Thoroughly mix the dressing
ingredients together and either coat the vegetables with it or
serve separately.   (*Serves 6*)

Sausage and Pasta Salad with Remoulade Sauce

1lb/500g chipolata sausages
8oz/225g pasta shells
Salt
4oz/100g cooked green peas
4oz/100g cooked French beans
3–4 tomatoes
1 small green pepper
8–12 pimento-stuffed Spanish olives

Grill or fry the sausages until crisp and brown all over.
Drop the pasta shells into 2 quarts boiling water with 2
rounded teaspoons of salt and cook for 12–14 minutes until
just tender. Drain thoroughly in a colander. Mix the cooked
peas and beans and sliced tomatoes with sufficient
Remoulade Sauce to moisten well. Pile in the pasta and
vegetable mixture. Arrange the sausages on top. Cut the
pepper in half and remove the stem, seeds and membrane.
Slice thinly and add to the salad. Cut the olives in half and
scatter over the top.   (*Serves 4*)

Remoulade Sauce

2–3 teaspoons French mustard
$\frac{1}{2}$ pint/300ml mayonnaise

1 teaspoon chopped capers
2 dessertspoons chopped fresh parsley
Lemon juice to taste

Blend the mustard into the mayonnaise. Add the capers
and parsley and sharpen to taste with lemon juice.

If one of these salads forms the basis for the meal, take
an energy- and warmth-producing fruit loaf, cake or tea
bread that makes a portable substitute for a dessert. Or it
can make a mid-afternoon snack with a hot drink from a
flask.

Spiced Nut Cake

9oz/250g self-raising flour
1 level teaspoon mixed spice
½ level teaspoon ground ginger
6oz/175g butter
3oz/75g soft brown sugar
2 tablespoons black treacle
3 eggs
1oz/25g stem ginger, drained and chopped
1oz/25g shelled walnuts, finely chopped
4 tablespoons milk

Grease and line a 8in/20cm round cake tin. Sift together
flour, spice and ground ginger. Beat butter, sugar and treacle
together until light and creamy. Blend eggs and gradually
beat into creamed mixture a little at a time. Fold in sifted
flour, stem ginger, nuts and finally milk. Turn into prepared
tin. Bake for about 1 hour at 325°F/170°C/Gas 3. Allow
to cool slightly before turning out of tin.

Celery and Peanut Teabread

8oz/225g self-raising flour
½ level teaspoon salt
Pepper
¼ level teaspoon garlic powder
1oz/25g butter or margarine

1 egg
¼ pint/150ml milk
2 stalks celery, finely chopped
3oz/75g crunchy peanut butter
1oz/25g peanuts

Mix flour, salt, a little pepper and the garlic powder and rub
in butter or margarine. Beat egg and milk together. Add
celery, peanut butter, beaten egg and milk to flour mixture
and mix to a soft dough. Spoon into a greased 1lb/500g
loaf tin, level surface and sprinkle peanuts on top. Bake at
375°F/190°C/Gas 5 for 45–50 minutes, until well-risen and
golden brown. Cover top with foil if peanuts become too
brown.

Barm Brack

¾ pint/425ml cold tea, without milk
7oz/200g soft brown sugar
12oz/350g mixed dried fruit
1 egg, beaten
10oz/275g self-raising flour

Put tea, sugar and dried fruit in a bowl, cover and leave to
soak overnight. Stir egg and tea mixture into flour until
smooth. Turn into well-greased 8in/20cm cake tin or
2lb/1kg loaf tin. Bake at 350°F/180°C/Gas 4 for about
1¾ hours. Serve sliced with butter.

Orange Tea Bread

4oz/100g margarine
10oz/275g self-raising flour
½ level teaspoon salt
3 tablespoons clear honey
Finely grated rind of 1 orange
2oz/50g walnuts, chopped
1 egg
4 tablespoons milk
2 tablespoons marmalade

Place all the ingredients in a mixing bowl and beat together
with a wooden spoon until well mixed (2–3 minutes). Place
in a 2lb/1kg loaf tin, previously bottom-lined with
greaseproof paper and brushed with melted margarine.
Bake on the middle shelf of a preheated moderate oven
(350°F/180°C/Gas 4) for $1\frac{1}{4}$–$1\frac{1}{2}$ hours. Leave in the tin for
2–3 minutes. Turn out and cool on a wire rack. Serve sliced
and spread with butter.

Picnic Cake is handy made in a 4-portion foil freezer tray
ready to take travelling.

Picnic Cake

4oz/100g butter
4oz/100g soft brown sugar
2 eggs
4oz/100g self-raising flour
2 bananas
1oz/25g walnuts

Cream together the butter and sugar. Beat in the eggs and
fold in flour. Add mashed bananas and chopped walnuts.
Then bake in the oven at 350°F/180°C/Gas 4 for 40–50
minutes. Cool and overwrap with foil.

Chocolate Coconut Slices

6oz/175g plain dessert chocolate
4oz/100g butter
8oz/225g castor sugar
2 eggs
4oz/100g ground rice
4oz/100g desiccated coconut
4oz/100g sultanas
4oz/100g glacé cherries

Melt the chocolate in a bowl over hot water and spread over
a greased, lined Swiss roll tin. Leave to cool. Cream the
butter and sugar until soft and beat in the eggs. Fold in the

47

rice and coconut, sultanas and chopped cherries. Spread over the chocolate and cook at 325°F/170°C/Gas 3 for 30 minutes. Leave in tin until cooled, chill in refrigerator and cut into fingers.

5

Meals on the Move

Not all *al fresco* feasts are purely for pleasure. Many are necessitated by modern travel – long cross-country drives for business or on holiday; train, coach and even air travel, all can demand adequate provisions. But not everyone prepares food to take travelling. Most people rely on (often inadequate) facilities *en route*. A pub may be fine for a light lunch, but its opening times can be inconvenient and it may not serve coffee for drivers. Also it may well be crowded, with stand-up eating only.

A thoughtfully prepared meal, taken in a quiet lay-by – or, better, beside a pleasant country lane – with flask of hot coffee or tea, relaxes the driver. Experts say that on long drives both passengers and driver need a break, preferably with a hot or cold soft drink, every two hours.

Cookery books don't usually mention that in certain conditions foods make one sick, but it's wise to think ahead.

49

Children may be subject to car sickness and should not be given over-sweet or fizzy drinks, chocolate or too much ice-cream. Boiled sweets and fresh fruit are better.

Before leaving home don't serve too rich a breakfast; avoid fatty and fried foods, even milk, and keep foods simple and light. Boiled or scrambled eggs are suitable.

Taking food on other kinds of journey saves worry and is an economy. A cardboard lunch box packed with light, non-thirst-making food can be eaten in trains, long distance buses or on a ferry.

Airlines provide meals on most flights, and their cuisine has been much criticised for being 'plasticised'. Actually, considering the limitations of food having to travel round the world in cramped conditions, they do pretty well. Foods with a reasonable amount of liquid in them are the best travellers; prawn cocktails and casseroles are good airline travellers.

America has recently seen a trend towards taking food on planes. Some travellers arrange with Chinese restaurants for take-out meals; some airports have take-out counters. The airlines don't like it but can't stop it, though in the States you can't take your own alcohol along. Here, when fellow fliers are trying to attract attention for a drinks order and one is hungry after long delays, it's satisfying to take out a pack of, say, smoked salmon with fresh brown bread, half a bottle of white wine or Champagne and fresh fruit, the last being something airlines seldom think of providing. Your own good strong coffee with proper cream is a blessing too. You can add to your own food anything fanciable from the airline's tray and use their cutlery and plates.

In past centuries it was customary for travellers to carry their own food, particularly when inns served poor meals. In 1850 the Simplon post hotel was described as 'dear and dirty, damp sheets, hard bread, hard water, old hens and of course hard eggs'. Today, with hotels cutting services, especially room service, as much as possible, the traveller may feel justified in taking his own sustenance. Arriving late, especially in country areas, it's disappointing to find that the chef has gone home, and that it takes infinite persuasion to get a sandwich sent up to one's room. Little wonder that Arabs, used to the nomadic life, sometimes bring small cooking stoves into hotel rooms.

Travelling by car, it's easy to take a hot meal cooking in a vacuum flask (see Chapter 7), fresh bread, wine and other foods. Staying near a shopping area, you'll find that most supermarkets – especially their deli-counters – provide basics for a room feast: pâtés, bread rolls, butter, cold cooked meats, salad items and fruit, even drinks and paper plates, though pieces from a foil roll can be makeshift platters. The hotel will provide glasses, ice and increasingly tea- and coffee-making outfits.

I find the challenge of making do in hotels particularly satisfying, having gone as far as to provide a candlelit dinner with proper wine glasses, chilled soup, hot-cheese-sauced entrée, orange salad and coffee laced with brandy. And I have warded off over-efficient maids in Calgary when the bathroom had become a salad bar. Having boiled eggs in the kettle, I was chopping them with salad dressing and curry powder for an *hors d'oeuvre*; the leftover legacy of a camping tour.

Such resourcefulness is useful for a woman travelling alone who doesn't want to face glances in the dining rooms of business hotels. (The curiosity still aroused by a woman dining alone in a hotel is a hardy reminder of male chauvinism.) One's own diet-conscious meal in the room, with TV on or the latest magazine to read, is a pleasing self-indulgence.

In most of these travel situations there is somewhere reasonably comfortable to sit down and a table to eat off, so foods need not be too simple. Flans are ideal, though packing must be careful to avoid crushing. Dishes must never be dry; in the atmosphere of planes, trains and, to some extent, cars dry food will curl or crack and become unappetising while thirst will be increased. A fruity dessert is best to cleanse the palate.

When planning a motorway meal with children on board, kit up the car with large plastic bags which will take rubbish and can in crisis be used as sick bags and a damp towel or cologne-soaked tissues for wiping sticky hands and mouths.

Use clip-on car trays if possible, or a small, round, deep-sided tray for each eater, or large foil trays or separate lunch boxes.

An old egg box can be used, not only for hard-boiled eggs but for tomatoes and soft fruit so they will not be squashed. Use small disposable screw-top bottles for drinks, take extra soda water or plain water and use straws for easier drinking in restricted space. If the dog comes too pack water for him and perhaps some dog biscuits or a bone.

I never intentionally cater for animals on picnics but I have fed much passing wild life, from lizards on the cliffs of Gozo – they had a passion for English country cheese – to passing swans on idyllic Thameside picnics and impertinent birds, secure in their National Park in the Rockies, that dive-bombed the picnic table, and perched on the sides of plates, prepared even to seize morsels on their way to my lips.

Countess Marcelle Morphy, in a delightful book called *Picnic Snacks* (1933) took thought for the dog accompanying the picnickers. 'Make a few nice sandwiches with buttered brown bread, and in between put a little chopped, underdone meat, or raw meat if Fido will eat it. Most dogs love brown bread and butter and it is good for them.'

Fresh milk will go off more quickly in hot weather if it's jolted in a car, so take instant dried milk instead; a tiny sealed carton of long-lasting milk or cream is an alternative. Puddings can be packed in individual yogurt or cream cartons with lids or foil securely taped on.

For toddlers take boiled water and fresh orange juice. Baby foods in jars can be eaten cold with a spoon and 'finger foods' to include are rusks and small sandwiches with, say, scrambled egg filling.

Even on a cold day the car can be fuggy, and chilled soup is a good starter. Tommitaster is a simplified variation of gazpacho; Iced Mushroom Soup is thick and nourishing. For larger quantities the ingredients can of course be doubled up, or multiplied as necessary.

Tommitaster

1 clove garlic (optional)
2 large or 3 medium ripe tomatoes

2 spring onions
Small sprig parsley
2 mint leaves
1in/25mm cube cucumber
Worcestershire sauce
Salt and pepper

Crush the garlic and wipe juice round bowl. Skin and
sieve the tomatoes, put pulp in the bowl. Finely chop the
onions, parsley, mint and peeled cucumber. Add these to
the tomato pulp and stir well. Stir in a dash of
Worcestershire sauce and seasoning to taste. Chill, or
serve with an ice cube in the soup.   (*Serves 1*)

Iced Mushroom Soup

4oz/100g mushrooms
½ clove garlic
1 dessertspoon vegetable oil
5oz/142g carton natural yogurt
Chopped parsley

Keep one mushroom to slice for garnish. Put the rest
through a blender until they are puréed. Crush the garlic
and blend with the oil. Stir in the yogurt and the mushrooms.
When evenly blended, chill thoroughly. Garnish with
mushroom slices and chopped parsley.   (*Serves 1*)

Chilled Beetroot, Cucumber and Orange Soup

1lb/500g cooked beetroot
1 large cucumber
1 bunch (10–12) small onions
2 heaped tablespoons chopped parsley
Juice and finely grated rind of 2 oranges
1 tablespoon red wine vinegar
Generous ¾ pint/425ml cold chicken stock
Salt and freshly milled black pepper

Peel the cooked beetroot and grate them coarsely. Peel
and deseed the cucumbers and grate these likewise. (Do

not use a blender for this soup as it won't have the right texture.) Trim the spring onions and slice as finely as possible. Put all the ingredients together in a large bowl, retaining one-third of the stock so that you can adjust the consistency if necessary. *(Serves 3–4)*

Cold meats can be served in most travelling situations as people can sit upright to cut. Imaginative and piquant sauces prevent the meat seeming dry and add a lot to flavour. Cold fish fingers don't sound very alluring, but cooked, cooled and served with plenty of tartare sauce, or this Tomato and Onion Sauce, they make tasty roadway snacks. Cumberland Sauce is a traditional idea superb with cold lamb, pork or ham; it is also tasty ladled over a slice of pâté or with meat loaf.

Tomato and Onion Sauce for Fish

Fry 1 finely chopped medium onion in butter with 4 cloves, salt and pepper until soft and golden. Mix 1 small can tomato purée with ¼ pint/150ml water and add to onion. Add 1 level teaspoon sugar and cook gently for 5 minutes, stirring frequently.

Cumberland Sauce

For 4 servings, heat 4 tablespoons redcurrant jelly until slightly melted. Remove pan from heat and stir in 2 tablespoons port, 1 teaspoon finely chopped onion, finely grated rind and juice of 1 orange, 1 level teaspoon made mustard, a pinch of cayenne pepper and a pinch of ground ginger. Blend well and allow to cool completely.

A quick and sweet piquant lamb pepper-upper is created by whipping 1 tablespoon made mustard with 4 tablespoons redcurrant jelly. It also goes well with cold sausage.

Other saucy thoughts to go with cold sliced meats:

Fruity Mint Sauce

4 apples, peeled, cored and sliced
1 dessertspoon water
1 tablespoon clear honey
1 tablespoon sultanas
1 tablespoon fresh mint, chopped

Stew apples with water and honey until pulped. Add
sultanas and mix thoroughly. Continue cooking gently
for 5 minutes. Remove from heat, stir in chopped mint and
cool. Serve with cold pork or lamb.

Jiffy Jelly

3 tablespoons redcurrant jelly
3 tablespoons lemon marmalade
1 glass port type wine

Heat jelly and marmalade in a saucepan and blend well.
Add wine. Stir and gently heat for a further 2–3 minutes.
Pour into smallest-size fluted cake cases or bun pans. Chill
well. Turn out when needed and serve with tongue.

Sour Cream Pickle Dressing

5oz / 142g carton sour cream
1 rounded tablespoon mustard pickle
Salt and pepper
Milk

Mix soured cream and pickle together and season to taste.
Add enough milk to give dressing a pouring consistency
(leave out milk if using as sauce with roast beef).   (*Serves 4*)

Yogurt Horseradish Dressing

5oz / 142g carton yogurt
$1\frac{1}{2}$ teaspoons horseradish sauce
$\frac{1}{2}$ teaspoon lemon juice

Grated rind of $\frac{1}{2}$ a lemon
1 level tablespoon chopped parsley
Salt and pepper

Combine ingredients and allow to infuse in a cold place.
Serve with smoked fish or meat salads.

The following is a selection of quick sauces to make when
a speedy getaway is needed.

Beetroot Relish

Mix finely chopped beetroot with double cream. Well
season with salt and pepper. Serve with cold meats.

Green Pepper Sauce

Finely chop a green pepper, stir into whipped double
cream, add garlic salt and black pepper. Serve with cold
veal.

Devilled Sauce

Stir into whipped cream 1 teaspoon French mustard,
$\frac{1}{2}$ finely chopped onion and a little chopped pimento. Serve
with cold ham or herrings.

Include a fresh roll or piece of French bread with the meat
and supply flavoured butter, either already applied or in a
foil wrapping, to go with the dish.

Mint Butter

Cream 3oz/75g butter and 1 tablespoon freshly chopped
mint. Serve with lamb.

Curried Butter

Cream 3oz/75g butter and add a squeeze of lemon juice.
Shape and cut into slices; dip each slice in curry powder.
Serve with fish or eggs.

Paprika Butter

Cream 3oz/75g butter, shape and cut into slices. Dip the
slices in paprika and serve with chicken or beef.

As well as plain, sliced meats, pork chops can be cooked
with flavourings and served cold with one of the above
sauces or with a green salad.

Herbal Pork Chops

2 thick rindless pork chops
½ teaspoon garlic salt
Black pepper
Olive oil
1 teaspoon dried thyme
1 teaspoon fennel seeds
4 whole bay leaves

Score meat lightly. Rub garlic salt and pepper over the
surface. Brush with olive oil. Arrange herbs in a heatproof
dish and place chops on top. Do this an hour ahead of
cooking so the flavourings mingle well with the meat. Place
dish under grill and brown chops slightly on both sides.
Cover dish with foil and bake at 325°F/170°C/Gas 3 for
40–50 minutes. Pour off excess fat and serve with garnish
of tomato slices or chopped parsley.   (*Serves 2*)

Tintinara Honeyed Pork Chops

1 tablespoon honey
2 teaspoons made mustard
4 pork chops

Mix together the honey and mustard. Put the chops into
the grill pan and brush with honey sauce. Grill until golden.
Turn and brush uncooked side and continue grilling until
tender. Place each chop on a square of foil and spoon on
any of the sauce that has dripped into the pan. Allow to cool
before wrapping.   (*Serves 4*)

A meat loaf is good for any kind of picnic as it can travel in the container in which it was cooked and be easily sliced through.

Lamb Meat Loaf

8oz/225g bacon
1lb/500g leg or shoulder of lamb
8 tablespoons breadcrumbs
1 egg
1 teaspoon Tabasco sauce
1 teaspoon dry mustard
1 teaspoon honey
Pinch marjoram
Seasoning to taste

Line a 1lb/500g loaf tin with derinded bacon rashers. Mince the lamb and blend with all the remaining ingredients in a bowl. Pack into the loaf tin and bake at 350°F/180°C/Gas 4 for 1 hour.

Summer Sausage Loaf

4½oz/60g instant potato
1 packet sage and onion stuffing mix
1 onion, finely chopped
Seasoning
8oz/225g sausages
3 hard-boiled eggs
1 tomato, sliced
Grated cheese

Make up the instant potato and stuffing mix according to packet directions. Mix together with the onion and seasoning. Grease and line a small loaf tin with greased greaseproof paper. Put in half the potato and stuffing mixture. Arrange the sausages in two rows on top, with the hard-boiled eggs running down the centre. Top with the remaining potato and stuffing mixture. Cover with a piece of greased greaseproof paper. Bake at 375°F/190°C/Gas 5 for 1¼ hours. Allow to cool slightly. Unmould into an ovenproof dish. Top with sliced tomato and sprinkle with a little grated cheese. Bake for a further 15–20 minutes.

(*Serves 6*)

Cooked meat can be cubed and used in salads; or other safari salads can be made with a rice or pasta basis. Both are easy to manage in a car.

Wellington Salad

12oz/350g lamb from a cooked leg or shoulder
1–2 teaspoons orange liqueur (optional)
3 oranges, peeled
2 stalks celery, finely chopped
2oz/50g desiccated coconut
1 teaspoon curry powder
4 tablespoons mayonnaise
1 lettuce, washed

Cut the lamb into small cubes and sprinkle with the liqueur. Cut 3–4 slices from one of the oranges and reserve for decoration. Chop the remaining oranges and add to the lamb with the celery. Mix the coconut, curry powder and mayonnaise together. Add to the lamb mixture and mix well. Arrange the lettuce leaves on a serving plate and pile the salad on top. Garnish with the reserved orange slices.

(*Serves 4*)

Prawn, Rice and Tomato Salad

1oz/25g long-grain rice
2 level tablespoons salad cream
1 level tablespoon tomato sauce or ketchup
1 level tablespoon sweetcorn
2oz/50g prawns or shrimps (fresh, frozen or canned)
Thick slice of cucumber, diced
½oz/15g sultanas
Pinch paprika

Cook rice in boiling salted water until just tender. Drain

and rinse in cold water, and leave until cold. Mix together
salad cream and tomato sauce, then stir in remaining
ingredients, including rice. Serve with hard-boiled egg and
tomatoes.   (*Serves 1*)

Pasta Waldorf Salad

3oz/75g short-cut pasta
2 red apples
1 tablespoon lemon juice
2 stalks celery, diced
1 tablespoon raisins
Salt and pepper
2 rounded tablespoons mayonnaise
1 tablespoon soured cream
1 tablespoon walnuts

Cook the pasta as directed on the packet. Drain, rinse
with cold water and drain again. Core the apples and chop
into rough pieces, leaving on the skin, toss in the lemon
juice. Turn the pasta into a large mixing bowl, add the
apples, celery, raisins and seasoning. Fold in the mayonnaise
and soured cream. Mix well and turn into a salad bowl.
Chop walnuts and sprinkle on top.   (*Serves 4*)

Chicken–Fruit Salad

4oz/100g long-grained rice
4oz/100g cooked peas
French dressing
4 cooked chicken portions
Lettuce
Fresh grapefruit sections
4oz/100g cherries or strawberries
4oz/100g black grapes
2 peaches, skinned and poached
Watercress, cucumber and tomato to garnish

Feather Cream Dressing
1 egg white
5 fl oz/142ml carton soured cream

¼ pint/150ml good mayonnaise
Salt
2 level teaspoons paprika

Cook and drain rice as above, add peas and enough French
dressing to moisten. Chill. Take portions of chicken, each
in one piece, such as drumsticks or thighs with bone
removed, or whole or half chicken breasts. Arrange on rice.
Surround with crisp lettuce leaves, fill them with the fruits
and garnish with watercress, cucumber and tomatoes. Make
the dressing by whisking the egg white until very stiff and
folding in the cream, mayonnaise, salt and paprika. Place
in separate container and spoon over chicken or use as dip
on side of the plate.   (*Serves 4*)

Salads can be presented in a Tomato Chartreuse ring
which gives colour to the dish; or for a complete meal fill
the tomato ring with a Pasta Country Salad.

Tomato Chartreuse

Bare ½oz/15g gelatine
2 tablespoons water
15oz/428g can tomato juice
Lemon juice
Onion salt
Pepper

Soften the gelatine in the water. Bring one-third of tomato
juice to the boil, then pour it over the gelatine and stir until
it dissolves. Add the rest of the juice and the seasonings.
Pour into a lightly oiled ring mould and refrigerate until
firm.

Country Salad

3oz/75g short-cut macaroni
4oz/100g streaky bacon
2 stalks celery
2oz/50g stuffed olives

61

3 tablespoons mayonnaise
Lettuce

Cook the macaroni as directed, drain and refresh with cold
water, drain again. Fry the bacon until very crisp, allow to
cool and then crumble. Wash and finely chop the celery and
slice the olives. Turn the macaroni into a bowl, add the
celery, olives and mayonnaise, mix and then finally fold
in the crispy bacon. Carefully turn out the tomato ring,
garnish the dish with lettuce and fill the centre of the ring
with the Country Salad. Pack in large plastic container with
a lid.

Small salads are very attractive made in plastic containers as side accompaniments to the meat.

Carrot Salad in Gelatine

2 large or 4 small carrots
4 large tomatoes
1 packet chicken noodle soup
1 dessertspoon gelatine
1 bunch watercress

Grate carrots and thickly slice tomatoes. Cook soup
according to directions, using $\frac{3}{4}$ pint/425ml water, and leave
to cool. Melt the gelatine in a little boiling water and mix
thoroughly with the soup. Pour into a mould or individual
plastic containers and when nearly set, carefully place sliced
tomatoes around edge of mould and fold in grated carrot.
                                                    (*Serves 4*)

Cucumber Salad with a sour cream base is cooling and refreshing on a hot journey.

Cucumber Salad

2 medium cucumbers, thinly sliced
Salt
$\frac{1}{4}$ pint/150ml sour cream

1 tablespoon fresh lemon juice
Sugar
Dill

Sprinkle the sliced cucumber with salt and leave for $\frac{1}{2}$ hour.
Then gently press out surplus liquid – retaining only the
cucumber. Make dressing from sour cream and lemon juice
with chopped dill and sugar to taste. Mix with cucumber
slices and serve. *(Serves 4)*

Just as flans provide an ideal carrying case for a savoury
main dish, a plate pie is a fine way of finishing a light motorway meal, particularly for business people travelling on
winter days. If possible serve a miniature of cream in a
carton with it.

Rhubarb and Orange Plate Pie

10oz/275g plain flour
Pinch salt
2½oz/75g margarine
2½oz/75g lard
1lb/500g rhubarb
Small tin mandarin oranges
2 tablespoons sugar
A little milk

Sift the flour and salt into a bowl. Rub in the fats until the
mixture resembles fine breadcrumbs. Add just sufficient
cold water to bind. Knead very lightly and divide the pastry
into two. Roll out one half and line a pie plate. Drain the
tinned fruit and clean and chop the rhubarb. Mix the fruits
well together and fill dish. Sprinkle with sugar. Roll out the
remaining half of the pastry. Damp the edges of the pastry
bottom with a little milk and carefully put on the top piece.
Press down the edges firmly and trim with a knife. Pinch
the edges to form a pattern and make a hole in the top for
the steam to escape. Brush the top of the pie with a little
milk. Bake at 425°F/220°C/Gas 7 for at least 25 minutes
until golden brown. *(Serves 4–6)*

A fruit cocktail is worthy of inclusion for its refreshing qualities, and this one with its brown sugar sweetening gives needed energy.

Picnic Fruit Cocktail

8oz/225g dried apricots, soaked in tea liquor
Grated rind and juice of 1 orange
1 banana
2 apples
2oz/50g grapes
2oz/50g brown sugar
4oz/100g strawberries

Strain the apricots and put the orange juice and rind in plastic containers. Slice the apricots and banana. Dice the apples and halve and depip the grapes. Place the fruit in the containers with the brown sugar and strawberries. Seal and chill before the journey. Accompany with cream.

(Serves 4–6)

An individual or slice of cheesecake is another nourishing dessert for a meal on the move, but must be well wrapped in double foil or placed in a small foil tray with cling wrap cover.

Individual Cheesecakes

4oz/100g shortcrust pastry made with butter

Filling
2 eggs
1oz/25g sugar
Rind of 1 lemon and juice of $\frac{1}{2}$ a lemon
4oz/100g cottage cheese, sieved
5 fl oz/142ml carton soured cream
2 level teaspoons flour

Roll out pastry thinly and use to line 4 deep tartlet tins each 4in/10 cm across. Line with foil and bake blind in a hot oven 425°F/220°C/Gas 7 for 15 minutes. Remove foil and continue baking for 5 minutes.

To make filling beat eggs and sugar in a large bowl. Add lemon rind and juice, cottage cheese, sour cream and flour. Mix thoroughly and pour equally into the 4 cases. Place in a slow oven (300°F/150°C/Gas 2) for 45 minutes until set. Remove and chill.   (*Makes 4*)

A traditional, almost nursery-reminiscent dish is comforting away from home and these three are all good travellers. Summer Pudding could be made in mini basins enough for one or two people, or in a large pudding basin to be sliced and wrapped in foil or cling wrap for travelling. Yogurt goes well with it as a change from cream.

Stuffed Apples

4 large dessert apples
Juice of $\frac{1}{2}$ a lemon
2 tablespoons honey
2oz/50g sultanas
2 tablespoons sponge cake crumbs
1 egg white
2oz/50g castor sugar

Cut a slice from the top of each apple and hollow out the centres. (A grapefruit knife helps.) Discard cores and chop flesh. Mix with lemon juice, honey, sultanas and sponge cake. Replace in skins. Place on a baking tray. Make a meringue by whisking the egg white until stiff. Whisk in one teaspoon of sugar, then fold in the remainder. Spoon meringue over apples to make a cap for each. Bake at 325°F/170°C/Gas 3 for about 15 minutes. Cool and pack carefully – cream or yogurt cartons to fit the apple snugly are best.   (*Serves 4*)

Summer Pudding

1 small white sliced loaf
2lb/1kg soft fruit in season, e.g. raspberries, blackcurrants
    and strawberries
3oz/75g castor sugar

Grease a 2 pint/1·2 litre pudding basin. Cut crusts from
bread, then cut all but one of the bread slices in half
diagonally. Arrange whole bread slice in bottom of basin.
Reserve 8 triangles and closely overlap remaining triangles
of bread around the inside of basin. Wash fruit and pack
into basin in layers with sugar. Cover top with the rest
of the bread triangles. The basin should be filled to the
brim. Place a plate slightly larger than the basin on top with
a heavy weight. Leave overnight in a refrigerator or a cold
place. (If frozen fruit is used put it in a pan with the sugar,
cover and heat slowly until sugar has just melted, then pour
into bread shell.) Serve with cream or natural yogurt.

(Serves 6)

Raspberry Trifle

1 packet sponge cakes (6–8)
Raspberry jam
1lb/500g raspberries – fresh or frozen
6 tablespoons cream sherry
1 pint/575ml egg custard
5 fl oz/142ml carton double cream, whipped

Split sponge cakes into two and sandwich together with
jam. Put half the sponges in a container. Spoon raspberries
over them, arrange remaining sponges on top. Soak with
sherry. Pour egg custard over while still hot and leave until
cold. Whip cream and spoon over top just before leaving
home.

(Serves 4)

Custard for Trifle

3 eggs, leaving out 2 whites
¾ pint/425ml milk
1oz/25g sugar
Vanilla essence (optional)

Beat the eggs and add the milk (hot but not boiling). Beat
together. Pour into double saucepan over low heat and stir
until mixture thickens. It must never boil or it will curdle.

The custard is ready when the mixture clings to the back of a wooden spoon. Add the sugar, and vanilla if liked. Stir until sugar dissolves and pour into trifle.

With the custard one can serve glazed, sautéed fruits as a quick follow-up food. Fry bananas or apple rings and glaze with melted redcurrent jelly mixed with lemon or lime juice. Glaze strawberries and pineapple slices with apricot jam melted with kirsch or apricot brandy. Orange segments (saves peeling and smell in car) can be glazed with orange marmalade melted with orange liqueur or sherry. Soured cream can also be served with these fruits; combine it with brown sugar, vanilla essence and lemon juice. For energy-giving, pack dates with sliced oranges, double or clotted cream and pineapple jam in small cartons.

⑥
Desk-top Dining

A survey of London office workers shows that 80 per cent equate 'a packed lunch' with sandwiches, and at a Weight Watchers class I once attended a frequent plea was from secretaries and factory workers for midday food ideas that would not be stodgy.

The person who eats at his desk or, on a fine day, goes to the park, or takes a lunch box to school, needs protein content: eggs, fish, cheese and lean meat are suitable and fruit should be included. Sandwiches with jam or fruit fillings are not adequate sustainers, though President Carter is not alone in thinking peanut butter *does* have more protein. Schoolgirls, secretaries and, increasingly, executives are worried about weight, and the meal should be kept as light as possible yet supply energy. The simplest slimmer's lunch box could consist of hard-boiled egg, a carton of yogurt, some celery and one crispbread with a little butter.

The lunch needs to have eye appeal with contrasting colours and should be well packed in a lightweight, rigid plastic box to survive the commuter crush. Cities provide unexpectedly good spots to picnic: the parks; the tiny spaces between buildings with sculpture or fountains that New York is so good at or the graveyards like St Paul's, Inigo Jones' church in Covent Garden, or a park panelled with gravestones near London's Mount Pleasant. But most will eat in the office, so foods that can be eaten in comfort with knife and fork can be provided. Cutlery, plates and napkins can be kept in a desk drawer and there is usually provision for a hot drink.

Sometimes a specially busy day at the office necessitates a 'one hand' meal that can be consumed with phone or pen in the other. Brown bread sandwiches moistened with salad cream with meats and salad ingredients mixed together are a good idea. Club and slaw sandwiches are not too messy. My husband's office Mondays are days of non-stop pressure, and as he travels by car I occasionally provide a platter of brawn or cold meat arranged with chutneys, salad items and a ready-buttered roll, all under cling wrap on a paper plate. Somehow he strolls through Bloomsbury carrying not so much 'a poppy or a lily in his medieval hand' as brawn and spring onion in one hand, briefcase in the other.

Rather than one substantial dish, two or three lighter ideas can be grouped together. Pack each in a small airtight plastic box, padded out with paper napkins or a piece of fruit. Start with an *hors d'oeuvre* such as hard-boiled eggs with a plain mayonnaise sauce or this curry-flavoured one.

Curried Eggs

4 hard-boiled eggs
4 tablespoons mayonnaise
5 fl oz/142ml carton double cream
2 tablespoons curry paste (or to taste)
2oz/50g gherkins, finely chopped
1 tablespoon mango chutney
Salt and pepper

Shell the hard-boiled eggs and place in a medium-sized
plastic container. Whisk the mayonnaise, cream, curry paste,
gherkins and mango chutney together and season. Spoon
the mixture over the eggs and replace the lid for the journey.
Alternatively the eggs can be placed in small greased paper
dishes and covered with cling film.   (*Serves 4*)

Raw mushrooms are a quick-to-assemble starter and can
be prepared the night before.

Raw Mushrooms

1 tablespoon vinegar
1 teaspoon lemon juice
1 teaspoon finely grated onion
Dash Worcestershire sauce
4 tablespoons tomato juice
1 tablespoon chopped parsley
Salt, pepper and prepared mustard to taste
Up to 1lb/500g button mushrooms

Blend all the seasoning ingredients together in a large bowl;
add mushrooms, whole or sliced, and leave to stand in a cool
place for at least 1 hour. Turn with a spoon two or three
times while they are standing. Pack in small containers with
lid or foil cover.   (*Serves 4*)

Tomatoes are good travel containers for a nutritious
cheese-and-meat filling.

Savoury Tomatoes

2oz/50g butter
4 large firm tomatoes
4 × 4in/10cm squares of foil

Filling
1oz/25g butter
1 tablespoon finely chopped onion
2oz/50g cooked rice

2–3 dessertspoons grated cheese
1 thick slice cooked ham
Salt and pepper

Stand tomatoes on their stem ends and slice off top third.
Remove pulp, discard tough core and use pulp in filling.
For the filling, melt the butter in a saucepan and fry the
onion lightly. Stir in the rice and tomato pulp. Add the
cheese, ham and seasoning. Pack the filling into the tomato
'shells'. Replace top and wrap each one in buttered foil.
Bake for 20 minutes at 375°F/190°C/Gas 5. Pack in
individual plastic cups or yogurt containers. Cover top with
foil or cling wrap   (*Serves 4*)

Marinated Kipper Fillets with Cole-Slaw

These are made by skinning 2 kipper fillets per person. Cut
them into ½in/12mm strips and cover with 1 tablespoon
dressing made of cider and vinegar mixed. Marinate for
4 hours. Mix 1oz/25g finely shredded white cabbage and
some grated carrot with lemon juice and 1 tablespoon
soured cream. Drain kipper and stir into cole-slaw. Season
to taste. This can be eaten with small fried cubes of bread or
brown bread and butter.

A cold soup can be carried in round plastic containers with
well-fitting lids.

Maid of the Mountain Soup

1 avocado pear
½ pint/275ml tomato juice
½ pint/275ml water
1 dessertspoon natural yogurt
Salt and pepper to taste
¼ pint/150ml milk
½ × 5 fl oz/142ml carton single cream
Chopped chives

Blend or liquidise all the ingredients except the milk, cream
and chives. Gradually stir in the milk and finally the cream.

71

Chill thoroughly and serve topped with chives.   (*Serves 4*)

Lamb is a good meat for an office lunch and leftovers from the Sunday roast can be used in this recipe together with sage and onion packet stuffing to stretch it and give flavour. Other members of the family can have the pie hot at home for lunch while a generous slice goes off to work.

Lamb Pie

Pastry
4oz/100g plain flour
2oz/50g margarine
1 teaspoon salt
1 egg, beaten

Filling
12oz/350g cubed lamb from shoulder
1 large onion
½ pint/275ml stock
3 tablespoons sage and onion packet stuffing mix
Salt and pepper
2oz/50g mushrooms, sliced

Make the pastry by rubbing the fat into the sifted flour to resemble breadcrumbs. Add sufficient water to form a pliable dough. Use two-thirds rolled out to line a 1lb/500g tin and reserve the remainder for a lid. To make the filling, brown the cubes of lamb in a saucepan, adding no extra fat. Add the onion and cook for 10 minutes on a gentle heat. Add the stock and cook for a further 30 minutes. Add the sage and onion stuffing. Allow to cool. Pack the filling into the prepared case. Top with the remaining pastry and brush with beaten egg. Bake at 400°F/200°C/Gas 6 for 30–35 minutes. Cool and remove from tin. Wrap slice for office in cling wrap or foil and place in strong carton to protect pastry.   (*Serves 4*)

A simple way of serving luncheon meat is to slice a 12oz/340g can into 8. Dip in a beaten egg and 3oz/75g fresh white breadcrumbs; fry in melted butter until crisp and golden. Cool quickly. Serve with wedges of lemon.

(Serves 4)

Plain ham or pork slices will seem dull in the dusty atmosphere of office or school. Add a palate pleaser of pickled fruit made when the pear glut occurs, or a fruit mayonnaise.

Pickled Pears

4lb / 2kg pears
Lemon juice
2lb / 1kg granulated sugar
1 pint / 575ml malt vinegar
2 teaspoons whole cloves
2 teaspoons whole allspice
3 pieces stick cinnamon
1 piece root ginger
2 pieces lemon rind

Peel, quarter and core the pears and place in a bowl of cold water to which lemon juice has been added to prevent browning. Place the sugar and vinegar in a large saucepan. Tie the remaining ingredients in a muslin bag and add to the pan. Stir over a low heat to dissolve the sugar. Bring to the boil and add the pears. Cover the pan and simmer gently until the pears are tender. Remove the pears and pack into clean, warm preserving jars. Remove the spices from the syrup and boil rapidly until reduced by half. Cover the pears with syrup and seal (do not use metal tops as these react with the vinegar).

Fruit Mayonnaise

This can be made at all times of the year. For 4 portions peel, core and dice 3 eating apples. Peel and segment 2 oranges, dice 2 bananas and mix all together in $\frac{1}{2}$ pint / 275ml mayonnaise. Chill and pack in airtight boxes.

A chef's salad is a complete meal in itself, but should not have the dressing mixed with it until just before eating. Carry this in a separate screw-top jar.

Chef's Salad

½ cos lettuce
1 bunch radishes
2in/50cm length of cucumber
1 onion
8oz/225g cooked bacon
4oz/100g blue cheese
Pinch each of salt, pepper, dry mustard and castor sugar
4 tablespoons oil
2 tablespoons wine vinegar

Wash and cut lettuce. Wash radishes and slice. Slice cucumber, finely slice onion and separate into rings. Cut bacon into fairly thick strips, cut cheese in small cubes and arrange all ingredients in plastic container. Blend seasonings, oil and vinegar and carry in small jar.

(Serves 3–4)

Salad sandwiches give a needed moistness. This one uses both brown and white breads.

Apple Blue

2 slices white bread
1 slice brown bread
1oz/25g butter
½ an eating apple
1 teaspoon oil
1 teaspoon lime juice
½oz/15g blue cheese
1 tablespoon soured cream or salad cream

Butter bread and remove crusts. Remove core but not peel from apple and cut into ¼in/6mm thick slices. Toss in a mixture of oil and lime juice. Layer neatly on slice of white bread, top with brown bread, buttered side down. Crumble blue cheese finely and stir into soured cream. Spread carefully on top of brown bread. Top with remaining white slice, buttered side down. (*Makes 1 sandwich*)

A memory from the South of France is *pissaladière*, sold from stalls in the streets in the Marseilles and Toulon area. With its cooked vegetables on a scone base it makes a succulent slice to eat in or out of the office.

Pissaladière

2lb/1kg large onions
4 tablespoons salad oil or olive oil
14oz/396g can tomatoes, drained
⅛ teaspoon garlic powder, or 1 clove, crushed (optional)
Salt and pepper

Scone dough
12oz/350g self-raising flour
½ level teaspoon salt
3oz/75g butter
About ¼ pint/150ml milk
2½oz/65g anchovies   ⎫
Few black olives   ⎬ *for garnish*
                      ⎭

Slice onions and cook gently in oil in a pan with a lid. The onions should be very soft and puréed but must not brown. This takes about 40 minutes. After 10 minutes stir in the well-drained tomatoes. Add garlic if liked, and seasoning. To make scone dough sift together flour and salt. Rub in butter until mixture resembles fine breadcrumbs. Add milk to bind to a soft dough. Roll out to a rectangle 8 × 12in/ 20 × 30 cm and use to line a shallow greased tin. Spread over the onion purée and arrange anchovy fillets on top in a trellis design. Bake in a hot oven 425°F/220°C/Gas 7 for 30 minutes. Place an olive in the centre of each trellis.

(*Serves 4–6*)

Though a banana, apple or orange can be included in the lunch box for quickness, a small dessert packed in a yogurt carton or small plastic container balances the meal. Fruit Snow, a more elaborate version of the ready-made fruit yogurts, is delicious.

Fruit Snow

5oz/142g carton natural yogurt
8oz/225g fresh raspberries or blackberries
5 fl oz/142ml double cream
Sugar to taste
2 egg whites, whisked

Place yogurt in a bowl and add the fruit, reserving four for decoration. Add 2 tablespoons of cream, and sugar if required; mix well. Carefully fold in the egg whites and divide mixture between four individual containers. Whip the remainder of the cream, put a large blob in the centre of each dish and decorate with fruit. (*Serves 4*)

I have never liked rice pudding since boarding-school days, when in the reverse of the scene in *Oliver Twist* I refused to eat the grey gruel that masqueraded as rice. A teacher sat over me and my congealing plateload all afternoon. Eventually, to break the impasse, I forced myself to be sick over it, which removed both teacher and rice very fast.

I have never become entirely reconciled to the product since; but though cold, cooked rice sounds depressing; it does, in fairness, make a good office dessert spiced with preserves and cream.

Using cooked rice left over from a meal: pack firmly into a bowl, leave a few minutes and unmould; it will hold its shape – a ring mould is the best and most decorative or for individual lunch box portions use small cups. Fill the centre with, or pour over, blackcurrant jam and top with cream.

Using instant rice: cook as directed, adding milk, sugar and vanilla essence to taste. Layer in a bowl with black-

currant jam. Garnish with chopped nuts or crushed macaroons. Serve cold or hot.

Using tinned rice pudding: chill the tin well. Unmould
into a carrying container and pour over the melted blackcurrant jam; garnish with nuts or raisins plumped in gin or
brandy (boil spirit and add raisins for a minute or two).

Veiled Country Lass is a romantic title for a prosaic but
tasty desert. Layer sugared and buttered rye breadcrumbs,
whipped cream, raspberry jam and some grated chocolate
in a plastic container. Chill until needed. Alternatively, use
layers of white sugared and buttered breadcrumbs (one way
of using up stale bread) or crushed macaroons, and tinned
apple sauce.

For a sweet-toothed office executive, the easiest desserts
can be made of leftover biscuits, pieces of cake, sponge
fingers, macaroons or meringue. Toast these and serve in
small cartons with jam to choice and whipped or soured
cream.

A simple sweetmeat can be made with bread if the eater
is not too diet conscious. De-crust a slice of bread about
$\frac{1}{4}$in/6mm thick. Cover in a dish with milk mixed with an
egg yolk, a little castor sugar and vanilla essence to taste.
Soak for about an hour. Fry in hot lard till golden brown on
both sides. While still hot, sprinkle with sugar and drain
in a hot oven on greaseproof paper for a few minutes. Allow
to cool and wrap in cling wrap – or sandwich slices together
with jam to taste and perhaps a little whipped cream.

Small home-made biscuits to keep in an airtight tin will
cheer the tea or coffee break. Sablés are delicious, though the
sugar powdering may be messy on the desk. To make about
1lb/500g of the biscuits work together 4oz/100g butter with
equal quantities of flour and sugar and 1 teaspoonful vanilla
essence. Roll out very thin and cut in small rounds. Bake
in a hot oven on an ungreased baking tray until golden. Dip
immediately in castor sugar to coat both sides. Leave to cool
and store in an airtight container.

7
Meals in a Mug

The vacuum flask has freed portable menus from the dullness of cold meat and sandwiches. As well as hot and cold drinks, the wide-necked flasks – among the few things cheaper now in real terms than when first introduced – will take casseroles, curries, stews, soups, pastas and rice-based dishes. Even chops and chicken joints can be taken along on any kind of meal on the move.

An advantage of these flasks is that they also save fuel. A stew can be started off at home, partially cooked, put in the flask and carried away. The food goes on cooking within the flask, by reflected heat, and when picnic time comes it's ready to eat. As food keeps hot in the flask for about 8 hours it can be prepared in the morning and kept for an evening meal, on late arrival at a hotel for example.

For best results vacuum flasks should be filled to the top to prevent heat or cold loss. Use a plastic or wooden spoon to remove the contents as metal may damage the glass lining. If a stew normally takes 2–3 hours to cook on the stove, it can be cooked for 20 minutes at home and left, without further heating, on the journey for 5–8 hours.

Partially cooked vegetables and fruit can also be finished in this way. For Fruit Dessert cook 1lb/500g plums in a syrup of 8oz/225g sugar and $\frac{1}{2}$ pint/275ml water boiled until a thread forms when lifted on a spoon. Simmer for 10 minutes and place in heated flask. Reheat syrup and pour over fruit. Leave for 4 hours; the plums will then be fully cooked, will retain their shape, and can be kept hot for 8 hours.

A $\frac{1}{2}$-litre flask can be added to a picnic collection and is fine for taking along hot vegetables, rice or pasta. Turnips, carrots, parsnips and onions can be brought to the boil and simmered for ten minutes, then put into the flask for 3 hours, when they will be cooked. As well as saving fuel, vacuum flasks free cooking rings in a busy kitchen.

Half-litre and 1-litre flasks more than pay for themselves if they are used often instead of being stowed away between picnics. Use them to keep meal portions hot for second helpings and when members of the family are late in for meals. Excess boiling water from the electric kettle can be kept in a flask near the stove and used for hot drinks and cooking vegetables. A flask of boiling water will keep hot over-night for an in-bed cuppa made with tea bag or instant coffee in the morning.

Liquid-style dishes travel best and remain appetising, and it's always more pleasant to eat something with plentiful moisture. A hot or cold soup is an excellent outdoor meal beginner, but it need not be confined to *al fresco* occasions. The housewife in the midst of a spring cleaning day, moving house, decorating or organising a party picnics in her own home, and there is much to be said for a nourishing meal in a mug that's quickly eaten among ladders, dust sheets or cooking pans.

Vitality drinks based on yogurt are fast, hot-day variations of meals in mugs, fine for the great outdoors, for desk-top dining and car journeys.

Grapefruit Mint Cup

5oz/142g carton natural yogurt, chilled
¼ pint/150ml fresh grapefruit juice (if tinned or frozen use
   unsweetened)
1 heaped teaspoon chopped fresh mint
Cucumber slices

Whisk together chilled yogurt, grapefruit juice and chopped
mint. Pour into a glass or container and decorate with a
cucumber slice.   (*Makes ½ pint/275ml*)

Spiced Apple Drink

2 × 5oz/142g cartons yogurt, chilled
6 fl oz/175ml unsweetened apple juice
¼ teaspoon ground cloves

Whisk together all ingredients. Serve sprinkled with a little
ground cloves.   (*Makes about ¾ pint/425ml*)

Cucumber, Lemon and Tomato Soup

4 × 5oz/142g cartons yogurt
1lb 3oz/541g can tomato juice
Grated rind and juice of 1 lemon
½ cucumber, peeled and cut into ¼ in cubes
Salt and pepper
Cucumber slices
Lemon slices
Chopped chives

Whisk together yogurt and tomato juice. Stir in lemon,
cucumber and seasoning. Serve well chilled, garnished with
cucumber, lemon and chives.   (*Serves 4–6*)

My own favourite quick break from work which can be
made *en route* is to take along a flask of chicken bouillon or
hot consommé with a carefully wrapped raw egg (use a

portion cut from an egg box). Slip the raw egg into the hot bouillon and garnish with grated parmesan cheese. The egg can be beaten into the bouillon if wished rather like the Italian stracciatella soup.

Cold soups for picnic fare should be put in a chilled flask for the best results. Leave the flask in the refrigerator for an hour or two or overnight before filling. But the widest use for the flask will be to take along hot soups for chilly beach days and winter walking days. These can be garnished with big croutons of fried bread to save carrying extra bread, or take a French loaf, partially sliced and spread with garlic butter wrapped in foil.

For a winter picnic, any soup can be made more substantial by the addition of dumplings, which eliminate the need for bread. Add herbs to give extra flavour.

Savoury Dumplings

2oz/50g shredded suet
4oz/100g self-raising flour
½ teaspoon mixed herbs
Salt and pepper

Mix suet with flour, herbs and seasoning in a bowl. Bind mixture together with a little water to form a soft dough. Using floured hands divide mixture into about 6 equal pieces and roll into little balls. Simmer dumplings in soup for 15–20 minutes until cooked.   (*Serves 2*)

Another extra that turns a soup into a meal is meat balls, which go particularly well with oxtail, tomato and vegetable soups. This recipe is enough for addition to 2 cans of soup.

Meat Balls

12oz/350g minced beef
1 onion, finely chopped
1 packet sage and onion stuffing mix

1 egg yolk, beaten
3 tablespoons oil

Mix minced beef with chopped onion. Make up stuffing
mix according to packet instructions. Mix into the beef and
onion mixture and bind together with egg yolk. Using
floured hands shape into 8 meat balls. Fry meat balls gently
in oil until evenly browned. Drain well. Add meatballs to
soup and simmer for 20 minutes.   (*Serves 4*)

Other ideas for making soups more filling. Add grilled
bacon rolls or pieces to mushroom-flavoured soup. Add
3oz/75g soft cream cheese, cut in cubes, to a mushroom
soup; heat gently without boiling until the cheese melts.
Noodles or long-grain rice can be added to a chicken soup
base; or add 2 tablespoons peanut butter and 2oz/50g salted
peanuts and heat through in the soup. Leftover meat and
vegetables can be diced and added to most soup flavours.

Here are some substantial soups for colder days. Onion
and Sausage, and Curry Soup both freeze well.

Cauliflower and Cheese Soup

2oz/50g blue cheese
1 medium cauliflower
8oz/225g chopped onions
1¾ pints/1 litre chicken stock
Pepper
1½oz/40g butter
1oz/25g plain flour

Grate cheese coarsely. Wash cauliflower, trim off outside
leaves and cut into sprigs. Place in a large pan with onion
and stock. Cover and cook slowly for 10–15 minutes until
cauliflower is just tender. Purée cauliflower and stock in a
sieve or liquidiser, season with pepper. Melt butter in a
large pan, stir in flour and cook for 1 minute. Gradually
add the cauliflower purée, stirring all the time. Bring to boil
and cook gently for 3 minutes. Gradually add cheese until

dissolved. Adjust seasoning. Serve with croutons and
chopped parsley.   (*Serves 6*)

Onion and Sausage Soup

3 onions, sliced
2oz/50g butter
1½ pints/750ml brown stock
Seasoning
8oz/225g sausages, grilled and cut into chunks

Fry the onions gently in butter for 5 minutes. Add the stock
and seasoning. Bring to the boil and simmer for 40 minutes.
Add the sausage to the hot soup and heat through. Fried
breadcrumbs and finely grated cheese can be taken along to
add to the soup when served.   (*Serves 4*)

Curry Soup

1lb/500g parsnips, peeled and diced
1oz/25g butter
1 cooking apple, peeled and sliced
½ tablespoon curry powder
½ pint/275ml cider (reduced to ¼ pint/150ml by boiling
    rapidly)
¼ pint/150ml beef stock
½ clove garlic

Put the parsnips in a large saucepan and cover with water.
Bring to the boil and simmer for 1½ hours. Allow to cool
but do not strain off the liquid. In another saucepan melt the
butter and gently fry the apple until tender but not brown.
Add the curry powder and stir in the cider and stock.
Simmer for about 1½ hours. Liquidise or sieve the cooked
parsnips and pour into the curry mixture. Reheat and season
to taste.   (*Serves 5*)

Florentine Soup

1 onion, sliced
1½oz/40g butter
1 pint/575ml stock
Grated rind of 1 lemon
11oz/311g packet frozen chopped spinach
3oz/75g broad noodles, tagliatelli, spaghetti or vermicelli
Seasoning

Fry the onion in butter for 3 minutes. Add the stock, grated
lemon rind and frozen spinach. (There is no need to thaw.)
Simmer for 20 minutes. Add the noodles and simmer for a
further 6–8 minutes (or 3 minutes for vermicelli). Season
to taste. Serve the soup topped with triangles of cold
scrambled egg on toast.   (*Serves 4–6*)

Apple and Leek Soup

1lb/500g leeks
1lb/500g apples – dessert or cooking
8oz/225g potatoes
1 parsnip (optional)
2oz/50g butter or margarine
1 pint/575ml white stock
1 level teaspoon savory or marjoram
Salt and ground black pepper
5 fl oz/142ml single cream
2 dessertspoons chopped watercress leaves or fresh parsley

Trim leeks, leaving 2in/5 cm of green above white part.
Clean well and slice thinly. Peel, core and slice apples. Peel
and dice potatoes; prepare parsnip if using. Heat butter and
fry vegetables and apples over gentle heat until softened.
Keep lid on pan and stir frequently. Add stock and
seasoning, cover and simmer for 1 hour or until potatoes
are soft. Liquidise mixture; if necessary thin with a little
extra stock and make quantity up to 1¾ pints/1 litre.
Gradually stir in cream. Add watercress or parsley and
adjust the seasoning. If a parsnip has not been used and the

soup seems sharp, sweeten to taste. Bring to simmer and pour into warmed vacuum flask. The soup can also be served cold, but do not freeze it. *(Serves 4–6)*

Smoked Haddock Soup

7½oz/215g frozen smoked haddock
1oz/25g butter
1 medium onion, finely chopped
½oz/15g flour
¾ pint/425ml milk
½ pint/150ml water
1 tablespoon chopped parsley
½ teaspoon lemon juice
Salt and pepper

Cook the haddock according to instructions. Meanwhile melt the butter in a pan and fry the onion gently. Remove pan from heat and stir in the flour. Blend in the milk and water, return to the heat and bring to the boil, stirring. Add the liquor from the smoked haddock and remove the skin from the fish. Flake the haddock finely and add to the soup with parsley, lemon juice and seasoning. Bring to the boil and simmer gently for 10 minutes. *(Serves 4–5)*

Frozen vegetables and tinned soup can be used as bases to create quicker soups.

Chicken Broccoli Soup

9oz/255g packet frozen broccoli spears
1 chicken stock cube
½ pint/275ml milk
5 fl oz/142ml carton double cream
10½oz/298g can condensed cream of chicken soup
Salt and pepper

Cook the broccoli according to instructions, but use the stock cube instead of salting the water. Drain well, reserving ½ pint/275ml of the liquid and place the broccoli, liquid, milk, cream and undiluted soup in a liquidiser. Blend until smooth. Return to the pan and heat through but do not boil. Season to taste. *(Serves 4–6)*

Green Pea Soup

10oz/283g packet frozen peas
$\frac{3}{4}$oz/25g margarine
$\frac{3}{4}$oz/25g flour
1 pint/575ml milk
Salt and pepper
2 teaspoons lemon juice

Simmer the peas in $\frac{1}{2}$ pint/275ml boiling water for 10 minutes. Meanwhile make a white sauce with the margarine, flour and milk. Purée the peas, saving the cooking liquid. Mix the purée, water and white sauce together and season well. Just before serving add the lemon juice. *(Serves 4)*

The transatlantic chowder is thicker than our usual soups, with chunks of potato, local fish or vegetables in a creamy base. These variations again provide the complete meal-in-a-mug formula.

Corn Chowder

10oz/283g can condensed cream of chicken soup
7oz/198g can drained, flaked tuna
10$\frac{1}{2}$oz/290g creamed corn
$\frac{1}{2}$ pint/275ml water
1 tablespoon Worcestershire sauce
$\frac{1}{4}$ teaspoon salt
Pepper

Put soup in pan with tuna and corn. Blend in water and Worcestershire sauce. Bring slowly to simmering point. Cook for 5 minutes, stirring occasionally. Add seasoning before serving. *(Serves 4)*

Salmon Chowder

1 packet mushroom soup
12oz/350g diced vegetables
1 small can salmon
3 sliced hard-boiled eggs

Make up the packet of mushroom soup as directed. Add
the diced vegetables; cook for 15–20 minutes. Add flaked
salmon and hard-boiled eggs. Heat for a few minutes.
Garnish with a slice of lemon.   (*Serves 4*)

CASSEROLES TO CARRY

Virtually any recipe from a casserole cook book can go
along happily in a vacuum flask. On the spot, or to make a
movable meal in a hurry, just mix together cans of baked
beans, tomato soup, corned beef and peeled tomatoes, season
to taste and serve from camp stove, or at home pour into
heated flask and put in the picnic pack.

An *All-in-one-stew-pot* can also be made from store-
cupboard cans in minutes. For 4 servings, mix together a
15oz/428g can of minced steak in gravy, 1 can diced new
potatoes, 1 can drained, mixed vegetables and 1 small can
whole peeled tomatoes. Mix all ingredients together and
bring to the boil. Simmer for 15 minutes, stirring occasionally, then transfer to a flask.

Chicken, often a dull-tasting meat, can be given flavour
with curry treatment as in Chicken Simla.

Chicken Simla

1 Spanish onion
3oz/75g butter
1 tablespoon curry powder
2oz/50g flour
1 pint/575ml chicken stock
Pinch cayenne pepper

$\frac{1}{8}$ teaspoon ground ginger
2 tablespoons mango chutney
12oz/350g cooked chicken
8oz/225g short-cut pasta (macaroni, spirals, shells etc)
2 tablespoons sultanas
5 fl oz/142ml soured cream

Finely chop the onion. Melt two-thirds of the butter and fry the onion until soft. Stir in the curry powder and flour and cook for 1 minute. Gradually blend in the stock, bring to the boil, then add the cayenne and ginger. Chop the mango chutney and stir it into the sauce. Continue simmering for 15 minutes.

Dice or shred the chicken. Cook the pasta. Add the chicken and sultanas to the sauce and simmer gently for a further 5 minutes, then stir in the soured cream and remove from the heat. Drain the pasta and add the remaining butter; toss to melt the butter. Place the pasta in a heated flask and spoon over the chicken.   (*Serves 4*)

Belly pork is an economical joint and can be used with baked beans to make a hotpot suitable for colder days.

Pork and Bean Hotpot

About 1$\frac{1}{2}$lb/700g belly pork
$\frac{1}{2}$oz/15g butter
1 large onion, sliced
15$\frac{3}{4}$oz/447g tin baked beans
8oz/225g tin tomatoes
$\frac{1}{2}$ level teaspoon dried sage
2 level tablespoons tomato sauce or ketchup
Salt and pepper
1 teaspoon cornflour
1 tablespoon cold water

Remove rind and bones from meat and cut meat into cubes. Melt butter and fry onion and meat for a few minutes until meat is browned on all sides. Turn meat and onion into an ovenproof casserole dish, add baked beans, tomatoes, sage, tomato sauce and seasoning. Mix well. Cover with a well-fitting lid and cook at 325°F/170°C/Gas 3 for 1¼ hours. Blend cornflour and water together and stir into casserole. Return to oven for 5–10 minutes until thickened. Place in vacuum flask. (*Serves 4*)

In Ireland in the old days, this dish was called Dublin Codell and cooked over a peat fire on the cottage hearth. Again it's more suitable for a colder day.

Irish Sausage and Potato Pot

1lb/500g sausages
12oz/350g onion
1lb/500g potatoes
¾ pint/425ml milk
Salt to taste
Chopped parsley

Prick the sausages with a fork. Peel and slice the onions. Peel and quarter the potatoes. Put these ingredients in a deep saucepan with a thick base, add the milk and bring slowly to the boil. Simmer very gently over a low heat for 1½ hours or until the potatoes are soft and breaking up. Stir carefully from time to time to prevent food sticking to the bottom of the pan. If a wide saucepan is used the milk will evaporate quicker and it may be necessary to add a little more. When the contents of the pan have become a thick creamy stew, it is ready. The spicy sausage seasoning will flavour the gravy, but you may wish to add a little more salt. Garnish with chopped fresh parsley. (*Serves 4*)

Spaghetti and rice are good ingredients to make meat go further in a casserole-style dish and again mean no extra bread is required. Spaghetti Mexicano is a spicier version of Bolognese, which can be served from a flask provided the spaghetti has been broken into manageable lengths before cooking.

Spaghetti Mexicano

2 tablespoons cooking oil
1lb/500g minced beef
2 medium onions, chopped
1 clove garlic, chopped
4oz/100g mushrooms, sliced
14oz/396g can tomatoes
2 tablespoons tomato purée
¾ teaspoon Tabasco sauce
¼ pint/150ml water
½ teaspoon salt
1 bay leaf
Pinch thyme
1 teaspoon Worcestershire sauce
8oz/225g spaghetti, broken into short lengths

Heat oil in saucepan. Add beef, onion and garlic and brown
lightly. Stir in mushrooms, tomatoes, tomato purée, Tabasco,
water, salt, bay leaf, thyme and Worcestershire sauce. Bring
to boil, reduce heat and simmer for 30 minutes. Meanwhile,
cook spaghetti in boiling salted water for about 15 minutes.
Drain spaghetti and mix with sauce in a flask.   (*Serves 4*)

Mad Haddock Kedgeree

8oz/225g cooked smoked fillet of haddock
10½oz/298g can condensed cream of chicken soup
6oz/175g cooked rice
2oz/50g grated cheese; or 2 hard-boiled eggs

Mix skinned and boned fish with soup and rice in a bowl.
Pour into a casserole and bake for 20 minutes at
450°F/230°C/Gas 8. Serve from flask sprinkled with
finely grated cheese or chopped hard-boiled egg.   (*Serves 4*)

Chicken Pilaff

1 onion
1 clove garlic

1oz/25g butter
1 green pepper
4oz/100g cooked rice
8oz/225g cooked chicken
5oz/142g packet frozen peas, thawed
1 tablespoon raisins
Seasoning
1 hard-boiled egg

Chop the onion, crush the garlic and fry in a little butter.
Add green pepper, deseeded and chopped, and fry for few
minutes more. Add rice, diced chicken and frozen peas.
Cook over low heat for 5 minutes, stir well, add 1
tablespoon raisins and seasoning. Serve sprinkled with
chopped hard-boiled egg.   (*Serves 2*)

Gammon and Vegetable Risotto

2oz/50g butter
1 large onion, peeled and chopped
1 clove garlic, crushed
8oz/225g rice
1¼ pints/¾ litre stock
Pinch of nutmeg
Salt and pepper
4 heaped tablespoonfuls cooked peas
1 red pepper, chopped and blanched
8oz/225g can sweetcorn kernels, drained
8oz/225g cooked gammon, diced
3oz/75g grated cheese

Melt the butter in a pan and add onion and garlic. Fry until
onion is soft but not coloured. Add rice and continue to
stir for 4–5 minutes until translucent. Take saucepan off
heat, add stock, nutmeg and seasoning. Bring slowly to the
boil, stirring all the time. Cover and allow to simmer very
gently for about 20 minutes, or until all the liquid has been
absorbed. Add vegetables and bacon and cook very gently
for a further 5 minutes. When serving scatter with a little
grated cheese.   (*Serves 6*)

IN THE COOLER

A home-made ice-cream served with sharp-flavoured fruit is a good end to a meal and can be carried in a chilled vacuum flask where it will keep firm for 8–9 hours. If the picnic is not far away the ice-cream container can be wrapped thickly in damp newspaper and kept in as cool a place as possible.

Vanilla Ice-cream

2 eggs
2oz/50g castor sugar
5 fl oz/142ml double cream
Vanilla essence

Separate eggs, breaking the whites into a 1½ pint/¾ litre mixing bowl. Put yolks in small bowl and mix with fork until thoroughly blended. Whisk egg whites until stiff. Beat in sugar gradually, 1 teaspoon at a time. Pour egg yolks into mixture, using a hand whisk to fold in gently. Whisk cream until it stands up in soft peaks. Using a metal spoon fold cream carefully into egg mixture to mix well. Add a few drops of vanilla flavouring, stirring to mix thoroughly. Pour mixture into a 2 pint/1·2 litre shallow container with fitting lid for freezing. This ice-cream takes only 4 hours to freeze and needs no further stirring or mixing.   (*Serves 4*)

8
Barbecues and Buffets

In Europe the barbecue is just becoming a popular way of cooking outdoors. In North America it's a weekend hobby, with some nostalgia for pioneer days, when portly Pa's get flushed with heat and alcohol, grilling steaks over smoking charcoal.

Barbecues are rarely elegant occasions. Eating food, charred and hot outside but often cold and uncooked inside, with sauce slithering round it, discourages the wearing of voguish clothes. The ideal dress is jeans and sweater or bikinis. The best barbecue I ever had was high in the Pyrenees, above Andorra, when a whole sheep was grilled over a fire (from time to time the Andorrans soused it with wine). A mountain stream nicely chilled the wine and later everyone lay about, replete, on rugs in a lush alpine field while the local police chief thoughtfully cooled the soles of the best-looking girls' feet with ice cubes.

93

A barbecue, more subtly, can be an adjunct to a patio buffet party. Small models like the Hibachi or the cast iron fogareiro, from Portugal, can stand on a table and grill small items. I'm not one for giant steaks and can never get my teeth properly around a hamburger and bun, but small, trimmed cutlets and mini kebabs can be very appetising. In the elegant Barbecue Room of the Corfu Hilton grills are recessed into tiled tables below extractor fans and guests select platters of raw meats from a buffet and grill their own. Sauces available include a cooling blend of cucumber, yogurt and garlic.

A barbecue can be as elaborate as you like, but for the occasional party a simple barbecue is made by stacking a few bricks in two piles and resting an oven grid across them. Make sure the space between the bricks has a firm dry base on which the charcoal can be burnt, or use more bricks to make a flat base. Line the base with double-thickness foil to make clearing up easier. An old metal wheelbarrow with a layer of stones could also be used. Another alternative is an old bucket with holes bored in the bottom, set on a couple of bricks with the fire inside and a grill across its top.

Charcoal is the best fuel and should be lit at least an hour before cooking starts. If the barbecue is big enough build the fire towards one end so that food can be moved aside to keep hot while the rest is cooking. Getting enough food hot at the same time is the main art of barbecue giving. Don't use petrol or oil to start the fire; rolled newspaper, wood chips, methylated spirit or fire lighters are preferable. When the charcoal is burning, spread the embers evenly, banking them down with old cinders when the heat gets too fierce. You'll need about 12lb/6kg of charcoal to cook a good meal for 15–20 people.

Utensils for cooking should be as long-handled as possible – a toasting fork is useful – and a pair of kitchen tongs and thick oven gloves, coming well up the wrists, are essential. Kebab skewers and thick paper napkins will also be needed. Keep a bucket of water handy in case of accidents and damp down the cinders when cooking is finished.

Foods suitable for grilling are usually also suitable for barbecuing. More economical barbecues can be made using cheaper grades of meat, marinating them well and cooking in kebab form. Fish, too, is excellent cooked over charcoal, and fresh herring can be cooked with mustard. Small whole trout and mackerel can be grilled with sprigs of fennel on them.

Always grease the grill to prevent food sticking. Use a large pastry brush to baste meat during cooking and to prevent too much fat falling into the fire. Foods must be kept moist, and oil, melted butter or these basting sauces will add flavour:

Guinness and Mustard Sauce

1 onion, finely chopped
2 tablespoons oil
1 tablespoon French mustard
$\frac{1}{4}$ pint/150ml Guinness
2 tablespoons clear honey
Juice of $\frac{1}{2}$ a lemon
Salt and pepper

Fry onion gently in oil for 5 minutes. Add the mustard, Guinness, honey and lemon juice; season to taste. Simmer for 5 minutes. This is particularly good with sausages.

Bitter Orange Sauce

5 tablespoons coarse-cut marmalade
Juice of 1 lemon
1 tablespoon brown sugar
Grated rind and juice of 1 orange
2 tablespoons raisins

Put all ingredients into a pan, and simmer for 5 minutes.

Food should be turned and basted on both sides. It is when the food is ready for turning that it should first be basted with the sauce, not in the initial cooking stages when the sauce could easily burn. Use long-handled tongs to turn meat rather than a fork which pierces it. Meats should also be marinated before cooking for additional moistness and flavour.

Throw a few herbs or dried orange peel on the coals during cooking to enrich flavours. And well ahead of the party add herbs like fennel, tarragon or thyme, to the oil to brush the meats. Add salt to the meats during cooking. If cooking in foil wrap, brush the inside of the foil with oil and seal well.

Cooking times, of course, will vary according to the fire's heat, wind and thickness of the food. A rough guide is chicken joints 25–30 minutes; 1in/2·5cm thick chops 12–18 minutes (turn halfway through); large sausages 4–5 minutes each side; hamburgers 5–6 minutes each side; bacon chops, gammon steaks or cod cutlets 5–6 minutes.

Marinade meats with this mixture:

Marinade

7 fl oz/200ml oil
$\frac{1}{4}$ pint/150ml vinegar or lemon juice
1 medium onion, chopped
1 clove garlic, crushed
1 teaspoon salt
$\frac{1}{4}$ teaspoon pepper
$\frac{1}{2}$ teaspoon dry mustard
Seasonings (see below)

Combine ingredients in a jar and shake well. Pour over the meat or poultry and allow to stand for 1 hour, or refrigerate overnight, turning occasionally. This amount makes enough marinade for 2lb/1kg meat or poultry.

Seasonings

For beef: 2 tablespoons Worcestershire sauce and $\frac{1}{2}$ teaspoon oregano
For lamb: 1 teaspoon curry powder
For pork: 2 tablespoons Worcestershire sauce, 1 teaspoon sage and a scant 2 fl oz/50ml soy sauce
For poultry or veal: $\frac{1}{2}$ teaspoon paprika and $\frac{1}{4}$ teaspoon each sage, savory (or marjoram) and thyme.

Barbecued Vegetables
Wrap vegetables loosely in heavy aluminium foil or in a
double thickness. Seal edges with tight double folds. Cook
on grill, about 4in/10cm from coals, turning occasionally,
or cook directly on the coals and turn often.

Potatoes
Brush each medium-sized potato with oil and wrap in foil.
Cook on grill or on coals for 45–60 minutes. To serve, cut
slits in potatoes through foil, pinch open, dot with butter
and season to taste.

New potatoes
For each serving wrap 2 or 3 small scrubbed potatoes in
foil with 1 teaspoon butter, 1 teaspoon chopped chives, salt
and pepper. Cook on grill for 35–40 minutes.

Sweetcorn
Spread each ear of husked corn with butter, sprinkle with salt
and pepper and wrap in foil, twisting ends to seal. Cook on
coals for 15–20 minutes, turning several times.

Onions
For 6 servings, cut 6 medium peeled onions in $\frac{1}{4}$in/6mm
slices and place on 6 pieces of foil. Top with mixture of
2 fl oz/50ml each of oil and vinegar, 2 teaspoons brown
sugar, $\frac{1}{2}$ teaspoon salt, $\frac{1}{4}$ teaspoon savory (or marjoram)
and dash pepper. Seal packages. Cook on grill for about
1 hour.

Carrots
For 6 servings cut $1\frac{1}{2}$lb/$\frac{3}{4}$kg peeled carrots lengthwise in
sticks and place on pieces of foil. Top with mixture of
1 tablespoon each brown sugar and lemon juice, $\frac{3}{4}$ teaspoon
salt, $\frac{1}{2}$ teaspoon nutmeg or ginger and 2 tablespoons butter.
Seal packages. Cook on grill for about 1 hour.

Mushrooms
Wrap whole mushrooms in foil with butter, salt and pepper.
Cook on grill for 20–25 minutes or on coals for 15–20
minutes.

Green or yellow beans
Wrap each serving in foil with $\frac{1}{4}$ teaspoon salt, $\frac{1}{8}$ teaspoon pepper and 1 teaspoon butter. Cook on grill for 20 minutes.

Frozen beans or peas
Slightly separate vegetables from 10–12oz/283–340g pack with a fork and wrap in foil with $\frac{1}{2}$ teaspoon salt and 2 tablespoons butter. Cook on grill for 25–30 minutes, or on coals for 20–25 minutes.

Kebabs
Kebabs, or shish kebabs, originated in the Middle East where nomads cooked meat on their swords over a campfire. For kebab-making use tender cuts of boneless meat cut in 1in/2·5cm cubes (2lb/1kg serves 6). Marinate if desired. Cook vegetables (such as tomato wedges, very small onions, mushrooms and green pepper pieces) with meat, or alone for 10–12 minutes. Season with salt and pepper. Brush with oil or marinade during cooking. To prepare kebabs, dip skewers in oil or rub with fat to keep the food from sticking. Thread meat and vegetables alternately on each skewer, leaving a space at each end so that it may be held or propped on the grill. Place kebabs about 4in/10cm from coals. Turn frequently during cooking. To serve, push cooked foods from skewers on to toasted buns or slices of French bread, or serve with hot rice or noodles.

Lamb and Kidney Skewers

$1\frac{1}{2}$/$\frac{3}{4}$kg lean lamb, cubed (cut from leg if possible)
4 lambs' kidneys, skinned and sliced
1 green pepper, deseeded and cubed
15oz/428g can apricot halves
4 tablespoons olive oil
6 tablespoons soy sauce
Pinch black pepper
1 medium onion, grated
3 tablespoons lemon juice

Put lamb cubes, sliced kidneys and green pepper in a bowl. Drain apricots and keep separate. Mix together oil,

soy sauce, pepper, grated onion and lemon juice and pour
over meat and green pepper. Leave for 1 hour. Thread
lamb, kidney, green pepper and apricots on to skewers,
alternating ingredients, and finishing with lamb. Grill for
20 minutes, turning frequently and brushing from time to
time with sauce.   (*Serves 6*)

Seafood Skewers

Marinade
1 lemon
$\frac{1}{4}$ pint/150ml olive oil
1 clove garlic, crushed
$\frac{1}{4}$ level teaspoon salt
Freshly ground black pepper
1 bay leaf

Kebabs
5 rashers streaky bacon, rind removed
$7\frac{1}{2}$oz/215g frozen plaice fillets, thawed
Salt and pepper
3 (6–8oz/175–225g) crayfish tails, peeled
8 large cooked prawns, peeled
1 large lemon, cut in 4 thick slices

Sauce
6 tablespoons thick mayonnaise
1 tablespoon tomato purée
2 tablespoons lemon juice
1 tablespoon Worcestershire sauce
1 level teaspoon grated lemon rind
1 level teaspoon finely chopped or grated onion
2 level teaspoons chopped parsley
Salt and freshly ground black pepper

For the marinade carefully pare rind from lemon. Squeeze
juice and whisk together with oil, garlic, salt, pepper, bay
leaf and lemon rind.

Stretch each rasher with the back of a round-bladed knife
and cut in two. Remove skin from plaice fillets and divide

into 10 pieces. Place each piece on a rasher, season and roll up, securing each with a cocktail stick. Cut each crayfish tail into 4 equal pieces. Place bacon rolls and seafoods in marinade and leave in a cool place for 4 hours, turning occasionally. Meanwhile prepare sauce by stirring all ingredients together. Season to taste. Leave for 4 hours before serving.

Remove seafood from marinade. Strain marinade. Cut each lemon slice into 4. Remove cocktail sticks from bacon rolls and divide with seafood between 4 long or 8 shorter skewers, alternating with lemon pieces. Place on barbecue for 8–10 minutes until fish is cooked, turning and brushing occasionally with marinade. *(Serves 4)*

Chicken Liver Kebabs

12oz/350g chicken livers
2 tomatoes, halved
1 onion, peeled and quartered
2oz/50g mushrooms
1 green pepper, deseeded and cubed
4 bay leaves

To baste
$\frac{1}{4}$ pint/150ml chicken stock
2 teaspoons vinegar
1 teaspoon Worcestershire sauce

Arrange all ingredients on 4 skewers. Combine basting ingredients and brush the kebabs with the mixture. Grill the kebabs for 20 minutes basting and turning occasionally.
(Serves 4)

If using chops or steaks, make sure meat is trimmed of excess fat which may burn, and brush well with sauces as required. Lamb chops are ideal barbecue fare with their little protruding bones which can be wrapped in foil for easier eating.

Barbecued Lamb Chops and Sauce

4 loin chops of lamb
Oil

Barbecue sauce
2 large cooking apples, peeled, cored and minced
1 medium onion, peeled and minced
¼ pint/150ml tomato ketchup
2 tablespoons brown sugar
2oz/50g butter
Salt and pepper

Place the sauce ingredients in a pan and bring to boil;
simmer 2–3 minutes. Brush chops with oil and grill over
glowing charcoal or under the grill, allowing 3 minutes each
side. Spoon a little of the barbecue sauce over the meat and
continue grilling for a further 3 minutes until sauce is brown
and sticky. Serve with remaining sauce.   (*Serves 4*)

Crispy Cutlets

10 best end of neck cutlets
Aluminium foil
2oz/50g walnuts, finely chopped
2oz/50g cornflakes, finely crushed
3 level teaspoons dry mustard
Salt and pepper
Flour
1 egg, beaten
Melted butter or cooking oil

Trim cutlets and scrape ends of bones clean. Wrap a small
piece of foil around each bone end to prevent it charring,
and also for holding it. Mix together nuts, cornflakes and
mustard. Coat cutlets in seasoned flour, egg and then
cornflake mixture. Dip in melted butter or cooking oil, and
grill over charcoal for about 6–7 minutes each side, or until
well browned and cooked.

Hamburgers are well-known barbecue food, but other meats: pork spare ribs, chicken drumsticks, sausages and even fish make tasty meals. Lambs' breast cut into ribs make an economical alternative to the spare ribs in this recipe.

Devilled Spare Rib Chops

1 level tablespoon made mustard
1 level tablespoon soft brown sugar
1 tablespoon melted butter
Salt and pepper
6 spare rib chops of pork
2oz/50g cashew nuts, finely chopped

Mix together mustard, brown sugar, butter and seasoning. Spread mixture on both sides of chops. Grill over glowing fire or charcoal for about 20 minutes or until tender, turning occasionally. Sprinkle chopped nuts over pork and continue grilling for a further few minutes. Serve with chutney and potato crisps. (*Serves 3*)

Spiced Orange Glazed Spare Ribs

3lb/1½kg meaty spare ribs

Marinade and glaze
2 tablespoons clear honey
Juice of ½ a lemon
Finely grated rind of ½ an orange
Juice of 2 oranges
2 tablespoons Worcestershire sauce
1 teaspoon soy sauce
Salt

Combine all marinade ingredients in a pan and heat gently. Simmer for 2 minutes. Cool. Cut spare ribs into serving pieces and place in a shallow dish. Pour over marinade and leave for 12–24 hours, turning occasionally. Remove spare ribs and place in a roasting pan. Reserve marinade. Roast spare ribs at 350°F/180°C/Gas 4 for 1 hour. When required place on top of barbecue grill and brush well with marinade. Cook, turning frequently and brushing with marinade, for about 10–15 minutes until well-glazed and crisp.   (*Serves 4*)

Chicken in Honey and Butter Sauce

2oz/50g butter
8 fl oz/225ml fresh or canned orange juice
3 tablespoons lemon juice
4 tablespoons honey
2 tablespoons chopped parsley
4 tablespoons soy sauce
1 dessertspoon dry mustard
6 chicken joints

Melt butter and combine with orange and lemon juice, honey, parsley, soy sauce and mustard. Wipe chicken pieces and place on grill. Cook for 45 minutes, turning often, and basting frequently with sauce, using a large pastry brush.

(*Serves 6*)

Barbecued Mackerel with Cider and Cucumber Sauce

Clean mackerel and run under cold water. Dry carefully. Score each fish with a knife and brush with oil. Cook over the barbecue for about 5 minutes each side.

Cider and Cucumber Sauce

1oz/25g butter
1 medium onion, finely chopped
4oz/100g cucumber (peeled and cut in ¼in/6mm dice)
2 level tablespoons flour
½ pint/275ml dry cider
Salt and pepper

Melt butter in a saucepan, add onion and cucumber and cook gently for about 5 minutes, stirring occasionally to prevent sticking. Stir in flour and cook for 1 minute. Remove

from heat and gradually stir in cider. Return to heat, bring
to boil, stirring, and cook for 1 minute. Add seasoning and
serve with barbecued mackerel. *(Serves 3–4)*

Too often the barbecue chef is more concerned with the
state of the meat than considering what to serve with it.
Transatlantic barbecues slip when succulent meat is just
slapped between two bun halves maybe garnished with some
salad. Vegetables and accompaniments that add warmth
and contrast to the meat are essential, and in addition to the
plain cooked vegetables mentioned above these help on
colder days.

Patio Baked Beans

4oz/100g brown sugar
1 teaspoon instant coffee
1 teaspoon vinegar
1 teaspoon dry mustard
½ teaspoon salt
1 onion
2 × 16oz/450g cans baked beans
4 slices bacon

Mix brown sugar, instant coffee, ¼ pint/150ml water,
vinegar, mustard, salt together in a saucepan. Cook over a
low heat for about 5 minutes. Cut onion in thin slices and
arrange alternate layers of onions and baked beans in a
casserole. Pour in the hot brown sugar mixture, cover and
bake for 15 minutes at 350°F/180°C/Gas 4. Slice the bacon
in 1in/2·5cm pieces and place on top. Continue baking for
another 30 minutes without the cover. *(Serves 6–8)*

Patio Green Bean Casserole

2 × 10oz/283g cans green beans
1 × 15oz/425g can cream of mushroom soup
¼ teaspoon oregano
Fried onion rings

Mix green beans, soup and oregano in baking dish. Bake at 350°F/180°C/Gas 4 for about 15 minutes. Sprinkle with fried onion rings and bake 5 minutes more.   (*Serves 4*)

Onions in Sour Cream

Cut a large Spanish onion into ¼in/6mm slices. Put in bowl of iced water containing 1 teaspoon sugar and refrigerate for 1 hour. To 1 5oz/142ml carton of sour cream add 1 tablespoon chicken bouillon crystals. When onions are well chilled, drain and toss in sour cream.   (*Serves 2*)

As a follow-up to grilled meat palate-soothing, fruity and creamy desserts are suitable. These can be taken from other chapters; but it is possible to barbecue fruits. A quick and simple idea that children, properly supervised, will love, is to have sharpened sticks for each guest who can then cook an unpeeled apple over the fire, until the skin peels off easily. Remove the skin and roll the apple in a bowl of brown sugar. Re-roast until the sugar caramelises. If available, skewer a whole pineapple, grill over the barbecue, peel and serve slices with rum and brown sugar.

Fruit Kebabs

Mix 2 tablespoons lemon juice with 6 tablespoons clear honey. Drain a 15oz/428g can pineapple pieces and a same-size can apricot halves. Cut 1 unpeeled eating apple in chunks. Alternate pineapple, apple and apricots on skewers and brush well with honey mixture. Grill for 5 minutes, turning skewers frequently and brushing with honey mixture, until apples are tender.   (*Serves 8*)

Minted Pears

Drain a 15oz/428g can pear halves and use 2 halves for each serving. Put pears, cut-side up, on a double thickness of heavy-duty foil. Chop 1oz/25g crystallised ginger and put a little with 1 teaspoon mint jelly in each pear. Wrap

pears and put on grill. Cook over medium heat without
turning for 10 minutes. *(Serves 4)*

Grilled Peaches

Drain a 15oz/428g can peach halves. Brush with butter and
grill, cut side down, until brown. Turn over and fill cavities
with butter and brown sugar, and continue grilling until
brown on the bottom. Pour a little sherry in the cavities and
serve with cream or ice-cream. *(Serves 4)*

Curried Fruit Compote in Foil

Pineapple slices
Fresh strawberries
Butter
Curry powder

For each serving place a pineapple slice on a square of foil.
Top with strawberries, add a little butter and a pinch of
curry powder. Seal and grill on a medium heat for 10–15
minutes. To serve, fold back foil and top with whipped
cream. This can also be used as an accompaniment to lamb
or chicken, served with sour cream.

Banana and Cinnamon Pancakes

Pancakes
4oz/100g plain flour
Pinch of salt
2 eggs, beaten
½ pint/275ml milk
Fat for frying

Filling
8–10 bananas (sprinkle with lemon juice to prevent
    browning)
1 tablespoon brown sugar
1 tablespoon cinnamon

Make the pancakes by sieving the flour and salt into a bowl.
Make a well in the centre, add eggs and gradually work in
the flour. Add the milk and whisk to form a smooth batter.
Leave the mixture to stand for a short while before frying
the pancakes. Sprinkle sugar and cinnamon over the bananas
and wrap each one in a pancake; continue until all bananas
and pancakes have been used. These can be served either
cold, or wrapped in foil and heated over the barbecue.

(Makes 8–10)

Sauces give a lift to plainly grilled meats. Some sauces
have already been outlined with their meats, but for a larger
barbecue party, make sauces in large bowls in a selection of
flavours and use some for basting the meat, others for
guests to add to their cooked meat.

Barbecue Relish

1oz/25g butter
1 onion, finely chopped
14oz/396g can peeled tomatoes
2 tablespoons cider vinegar
2 tablespoons demerara sugar
Worcestershire sauce
2 tablespoons sweet pickle
½ teaspoon French mustard

Gently melt the butter. Add the chopped onion and cook
until soft without browning for 5 minutes. Add remaining
ingredients, bring to boil, reduce heat and simmer for 10
minutes. Serve either hot or cold with meat, especially
bacon.

Quick Barbecue Sauce

2oz/50g butter
1 large onion
2 packets tomato soup
4 tablespoons vinegar
1 tablespoon Branston pickle
1½ pints/750ml water

Cook the onion in butter until transparent. Add the soup, vinegar and pickle and gradually stir in the water. Bring to the boil and simmer for 5–10 minutes. Serve with bacon, ham and meats.

Piquant Sauce

3 chopped gherkins
2 teaspoons piccalilli, chopped
6 tablespoons vinegar
1 small can condensed milk

Mix the gherkins, piccalilli and vinegar with the condensed milk. Serve with fish.

Horseradish Sauce

2 × 5oz/142g cartons natural yogurt
4 tablespoons salad dressing
3 level tablespoons horseradish sauce
2 level tablespoons chopped parsley
Pepper and salt

Mix all the ingredients together in a small basin and season to taste. Serve the sauce cold, as a dip for sausages, cubes of meat or fish cooked over the barbecue.

Pineapple and Cider Sauce

1 level tablespoon cornflour
½ pint/275ml dry cider
4oz/100g fresh or canned pineapple, chopped
1oz/25g seedless raisins

Blend cornflour with 2 tablespoons of the cider. Heat remaining cider in a saucepan, then pour on to blended cornflour, stirring. Return to heat and bring to the boil, stirring. Add pineapple and raisins, and heat through. Serve with gammon steaks, boiled bacon or pork chops.

Indonesian Sauce

1 tablespoon salad oil
4 level tablespoons peanut butter
¼ pint/150ml tomato ketchup
3 tablespoons Worcestershire sauce
Pinch garlic powder
¼ level teaspoon salt

Heat oil gently in pan and add peanut butter. Continue
heating gently, stirring occasionally, until peanut butter
begins to thicken and darkens slightly. Immediately remove
from heat and stir in tomato ketchup and Worcestershire
sauce. Season to taste with garlic powder and salt. Leave
for 2 hours before using. Reheat gently, adding a little water
if sauce is too thick. Serve with barbecued or grilled chicken
and steaks.

Chimichuri Sauce from Argentina

4 garlic cloves, finely chopped
1 sprig parsley
4 tablespoons corn oil
4 tablespoons vinegar
Pinch oregano
1–2 teaspoons chilli powder, according to taste
1 teaspoon tomato purée
2 bay leaves
1 dessertspoon salt

Place all ingredients in a bottle. Cork it and shake. Leave
for 24 hours before using, and shake before using to sprinkle
on beef during the barbecueing.

NOTE: Up to 1 pint of water may be added to the basic
sauce for basting meat. When meat is barbecued over a good
heat, a large quantity of sauce is required and the water
evaporates as meat sizzles. Chimichuri sauce can be stored

and water added as required for sprinkling over smaller meat cuts.

While the guests are waiting for the meat to be grilled, it's as well to have bowls of dips with crisps, pieces of raw vegetables such as celery, carrot and cucumber sticks and cauliflower florets; small cheese biscuits and chunks of French bread or garlic bread to stave off hunger pangs.

Piquant Dip

8oz/225g packet Philadelphia Full Fat Soft Cheese
3 teaspoons Worcestershire sauce
2 teaspoons lemon juice
Milk
1 tablespoon chopped parsley
Grated rind of $\frac{1}{2}$ a lemon
Seasoning

Cream the cheese until smooth, gradually adding the Worcestershire sauce, lemon juice and sufficient milk to form a desirable 'dipping' consistency. Stir in the parsley and lemon rind and season to taste.

PATIO PARTIES

On a fine evening or sunny lunch-time meals can move out of doors to a wind-sheltered area (with lanterns for the evening, hung high to attract insects away from the food). These outdoor 'buffets' should never live up to that name; arrangement of food in a small space is essential so that guests are not jostling each other and spilling things. Keep cutlery, crockery and napkins on a separate side table, separate the bar from the food and make the central food table a logical procession from *hors d'oeuvre* (if not served separately) to dessert so that no one drops mayonnaise into the jelly or is uncertain whether a pretty fruit arrangement is meant to be salad or sweet.

Food can be basically cold dishes made up in the kitchen at leisure, though some hot dishes can be added on hot plates and candle warmers. The new slow cookers with long enough electric leads are ideal for keeping dishes warm without burning during long parties. Even on a warm evening a dish of pasta or a homely macaroni cheese, its sauce perhaps spiked with curry and chopped frankfurter sausages, will be popular as a side serving with cold meats.

The best patio party I recall was in Norway. We sat on cushions spread over a wooden jetty-like floor above a fjord, watching the glow of the never-setting summer sun through an etching of pines. We ate piles of fresh prawns, peeling them ourselves, with crusty bread and butter and quaffed pints of chilled beer alongside slugs of fiery aquavit. Taped music played softly in the background, lights gleamed yellow in the log cabin behind us and the party ended with plenty of pastries, *gâteaux* and excellent Scandinavian coffee.

This was eating at its simplest and perhaps most enjoyable, and a pattern for patio eating here can be taken from Scandinavia. The famous Swedish cold table arose in days when a gathering was an important social occasion and each country housewife contributed her own dish to the feast. Cold food, with a few dishes kept hot on a plate, is the Scandinavian way.

People circulating and talking, arriving at different times, can't easily be catered for with lots of hot foods. Cold fork foods that go down better in a hot crowded room can be arranged on the table in advance.

A Scandinavian-type patio feast might be a selection of fish or piquant salads to stimulate the appetite, then smoked fishes and meats made into a series of mousses. Scandinavians often eat cold scrambled egg with these dishes; decorated with chopped chives this makes a good buffet side dish. The hot section should contain just one or two dishes; hot *quiches* are ideal and it doesn't matter if they get cold. Guests can enjoy slicing a big boiled bacon joint for themselves. Just as in Scandinavia there is a definite order of eating dishes, so the buffet should be arranged so that guests are not presented with a muddle of flavours.

Start with a selection of mousses perhaps backed with a bowl of *crudités* – cauliflower florets, halved button mushrooms, carrots and radishes. Or as an alternative to *vol-au-vents* make inexpensive bread cases from stale bread and serve hot or cold with a filling. These can be taken round on trays as the guests assemble.

Breadcases

18 thin slices bread, crusts removed
4oz/100g margarine or butter, melted

Roll bread with rolling pin until thin. Trim into neat squares or cut into 3in/8cm plain rounds. Brush both sides with margarine or butter, and place immediately in patty tins. Bake in a moderate oven (350°F/180°C/Gas 4) on second and third shelves from top for 20–30 minutes until crisp and golden brown. Fill as required. Serve hot.

(Makes 18)

Fillings (for 18 breadcases or medium *vol-au vents*)

1oz/25g butter or margarine
1oz/25g plain flour
½ pint/275ml milk
Seasoning

Melt fat in a medium-sized saucepan. Stir in flour and cook gently for 1–2 minutes. Add milk gradually, beating well between each addition. Bring to the boil, stirring continuously and cook for 2 minutes. Beat well until smooth and glossy. Add seasoning. Use with any of the following additions:

Asparagus
11oz/311g can asparagus, drained and chopped, pinch nutmeg, 1 teaspoon lemon juice.

Ham and Tongue
2oz/50g ham and 2oz/50g tongue, cooked and chopped.

Mushroom and Bacon
4oz/100g mushrooms and 2 bacon rashers, chopped and
    fried together.

Prawn
4oz/100g peeled prawns; 1 teaspoon lemon juice; 2
    teaspoons chopped capers.

Sweetcorn
8oz/226g can sweetcorn, drained.

Bread sticks are another bread-based item to make for the
first course of a party. They can be used with the dips.

Bread Sticks

Use 1–2 day old bread. Cut into ½in/12mm thick slices,
remove crusts and cut each slice into fingers. Deep fry until
golden, then turn out on to absorbent kitchen paper.
Sprinkle with onion salt while still hot.

Danish Blue Savoury

½oz/15g powdered gelatine
4 tablespoons water
4oz/100g Danish Blue cheese
5 fl oz/142ml double cream
2 eggs
2 tablespoons tomato ketchup
2–4oz/50–100g chopped walnuts

To decorate
Lettuce
Black grapes
Walnuts

Dissolve the gelatine in the water over gentle heat, stirring
all the time. Allow to cool. Finely grate or mash the cheese.
Beat the cream until fairly stiff. Separate the eggs. Mix the
cheese with the tomato ketchup, egg yolks and chopped

113

walnuts. Beat the whites until very stiff. Add the cool gelatine to the cheese mixture and gently fold in first the cream and then the egg whites. Pour into a well-buttered mould and leave in a cool place to set. Turn out just before serving and decorate with lettuce leaves and black grapes, adding a few whole walnuts if available. (*Serves 4–6*)

Fish Mousse and Sauces

1½oz/40g butter or margarine
1½oz/40g flour
½ teaspoon curry powder
¾ pint/425ml milk
Salt and pepper
Squeeze of lemon juice
1 tablespoon chopped chives
1 small can sweetcorn, drained
½oz/15g gelatine, dissolved in 3 tablespoons water
12oz/350g cooked cod
2 eggs, separated
5 fl oz/142ml double cream, whipped

Melt the butter, add flour and curry powder and cook for 1 minute. Gradually stir in the milk. Season the sauce with salt, pepper, lemon juice and the chives and sweetcorn. Stir in the gelatine. Remove the skin and bones and then flake the fish. Once the sauce has cooled and begun to set, blend in the flaked fish and the egg yolks. Fold in the whipped cream and stiffly beaten egg white. Pour the mixture into a fish mould and place in refrigerator until set. Serve with a selection of sauces. (*Serves 4*)

Curry Sauce

1oz/25g butter
1oz/25g flour
1 level teaspoon curry powder
½ pint/275ml milk
Salt and white pepper
1 tablespoon cream

Melt the butter and blend in the flour and curry powder.
Simmer for a minute or two, stirring continuously.
Gradually stir in the milk and cook over a gentle heat until
the sauce becomes glossy and of a coating consistency.
Season and stir in the cream.

Shrimp Sauce

1oz/25g butter
1oz/25g flour
½ pint/275ml well-flavoured fish stock
5oz/142g buttered shrimps
1–2 tablespoons double cream
Tomato purée
Salt and white pepper
Pinch of cayenne pepper
1 tablespoon lemon juice

Melt the butter, blend in the flour and simmer for a minute
or two, stirring continuously. Gradually stir in the fish stock
and bring to the boil, stirring, until the sauce becomes glossy.
Add the shrimps to the sauce and just before serving add
the cream, tomato purée, seasonings and lemon juice.

Cold salads with fish are ideal for summer evenings and
the Scandinavians, who serve marinated herrings on their
cold tables all year round, prove the weather does not have
to be hot to eat cold food.

After salads include some lighter hot dishes such as Meat
Balls and Jansson's Temptation, another traditional dish
from Sweden.

Meat Balls

1 teaspoon potato or ordinary flour
1½ tablespoons breadcrumbs
1 tablespoon grated onion
4 fl oz/100ml double cream
8oz/225g minced beef
2oz/50g minced pork

Milk to mix
Salt and pepper
Butter for frying

Stir the flour, breadcrumbs and onion into the cream and let the mixture swell for about 15 minutes. Mix in the meat. Add the milk a little at a time, stirring until the mixture is sufficiently firm. Season with salt and pepper. Shape into small balls and fry in plenty of butter over medium heat. Shake the pan often during frying so the meat balls do not lose their shape. *(Serves 4)*

Jansson's Temptation

6 potatoes
2 onions, thinly sliced
2 tablespoons butter
10 anchovy fillets
7 fl oz/200ml double cream

Slice the potatoes and cut into strips the size of a match. Rinse them in cold water and drain well. Fry the onion golden brown in the butter. Place half of the potato strips in a buttered baking dish, then a layer of onions, the anchovies and lastly the rest of the potatoes. Pour the cream over all and top with a few pieces of butter. Bake at 400°F/200°C/Gas 6 for about 45 minutes. *(Serves 4)*

To finish the meal, jellies, flans, cheesecakes, whipped creams, mini pancakes and fresh fruit look colourful and gleam in candlelight on the table. Jellies seem to appeal much to adults and are throat cooling among the cocktail chatter. A measure of port added to a raspberry jelly with fruit is delicious.

Lemon Whip

1 packet lemon jelly
¼ pint/150ml boiling water
15oz/428g can ready-to-serve custard

2 eggs, separated
Finely grated rind of 1 lemon
Mint leaves

Dissolve jelly in water. Whisk in custard, egg yolks and
lemon rind. Chill until mixture is cold and just beginning
to thicken. Whisk until foamy. Beat egg whites until stiff
and fold into lemon mixture. Turn into bowl and chill till
set. Decorate with mint leaves.   (*Serves 6*)

Pineapple Rum Jelly

12oz/340g can pineapple pieces
1 tablespoon kirsch
½oz/15g gelatine
3 tablespoons cold water
Juice of 1 lemon
2 fl oz/50ml rum
2oz/50g sugar

Drain the pineapple juice from the pieces. Add the kirsch
to the pieces and leave to soak for at least 2 hours. Dissolve
the gelatine in 3 tablespoons water in a basin standing in
hot water. Warm the pineapple and lemon juices. Stir the
dissolved gelatine into warmed mixture. Leave to cool.
When on the point of setting, add the rum, stir in the
pineapple pieces and kirsch mixture and pour into a wetted
mould. Leave it in a cool place or refrigerator to set.
                                                   (*Serves 4*)

Gingernut Lime Layer

1 packet lime jelly
8 gingernut biscuits, crushed
1 egg white
1oz/25g castor sugar

Place the jelly in a basin, add ½ pint/275ml boiling water
and stir until dissolved. Allow to cool. Put the crushed
biscuits into a shallow dish, then pour over ¼ pint/150ml

jelly. Leave to set. When the remaining jelly is just on the point of setting, fold in the egg white, beaten into a stiff meringue with the sugar. Spoon over the jelly and biscuits in the dish. Leave to set. (*Serves 6*)

Crunchy Raspberry Mousse

6oz/175g digestive biscuits, crushed
3oz/75g margarine, melted

Filling
7¾oz/220g can raspberries
½ × 1 pint/575ml packet raspberry jelly
6oz/170ml can evaporated milk
Double cream

Mix biscuits and margarine together. Press into bottom and sides of 8in/20cm flan dish. Chill. Drain juice from raspberries and make up to ¼ pint/150ml with boiling water. Dissolve jelly in this and leave to cool. When on the point of setting, whisk evaporated milk into jelly until light and fluffy. Add raspberries (reserving a few for decoration), and pour quickly into crumb case. Chill before serving. Decorate with raspberries and whipped cream. (*Serves 6*)

Apricot Fool

2 tablespoons natural yogurt
1lb/500g cooked, sieved apricots
2 egg whites, whisked
Chocolate curls

Stir yogurt into cooled fruit purée. Fold in whisked egg whites. Place in a bowl and chill, then decorate with chocolate curls. (Serve within 1–2 hours of making.)
(*Serves 4*)

German Cheese Pancakes

7oz/200g curd cheese
Pinch salt
3 eggs
Grated rind of $\frac{1}{2}$ a lemon
6 tablespoons flour
2 tablespoons sugar
1 tablespoon butter
1 tablespoon chopped almonds
Fat for frying
Sugar and cinnamon to serve

Mix curd cheese and other ingredients to a smooth batter.
Heat fat in pan and place small dots of mixture in pan.
Flatten and brown on both sides. Sprinkle with sugar and
cinnamon and serve with plums, cherries or cranberries.

(Serves 4)

9

Fêtes Champêtres

Whatever the benefits of plastic boxes, vacuum flasks, cling wraps, foil and motor transport, which have all made picnicking such a flexible and variable way of eating out, they have taken away some of the gloss and glamour characteristic of picnics of the past.

The Middle Ages loved a Maytime picnic with musical accompaniment and tables set out in a forest glade, a welcome relief from long chill winters of clustering round fires in baronial halls and eating preserved meats. But it was the Victorian picnic that's remembered for its size and solidity. Mrs Beeton, who left nothing out of her famous book, planned menus for a picnic for forty persons, and the food list includes a joint of cold roast beef, a joint of cold boiled beef, 2 ribs of lamb, 2 shoulders of lamb, 4 roast fowls, 2 roast ducks, 1 ham, 1 tongue, 2 veal-and-ham pies, 2 pigeon pies, 6 medium-size lobsters, 1 piece of collared calf's head, 18 lettuces, 6 baskets of salad and 6 cucumbers for openers. It then goes on to include plenty of fruit, pies, cheesecakes, 2 cold cabinet puddings in moulds, 1 large cold Christmas pudding, a few baskets of fresh fruit, biscuits, rolls, loaves, 2 plain plum cakes, 2 pound cakes, 2 sponge cakes and a $\frac{1}{2}$lb of tea! 'Coffee,' Mrs Beeton notes, 'is not suitable for a picnic, being difficult to make.'

Mrs Beeton left nothing to chance and added a check-list of necessities: 'Take three corkscrews and three or four teapots.' The three corkscrews came into play with the impressive list of 3 dozen quarts of ale, 2 dozen bottles each of ginger beer, soda water and lemonade, 6 bottles of sherry, 6 bottles of claret, champagne 'at discretion' and any other preferred light wine, and 2 bottles of brandy. The quantities work out roughly at three bottles of drink per head.

Today everything from the crinolines to the catering has been scaled down, but we still have the glories of champagne and cold salmon picnics at Glyndebourne, elaborate hampers taken from the boot of the Rolls at race meetings and school sports days. There are still picnics that are planned and judged as parties, the revellers dressed up and eating special foods. Such picnics take on something of Manet's painting, *Déjeuner sur l'Herbe*. The air is warm and still and nature is at its best and most floral. The dream ignores the realities of gnats, wasps, mud, inquisitive cows, car exhaust fumes, rain and traffic jams. In the mind's eye there is always a white cloth on green grass under a spreading tree. In life it's almost impossible to find a piece of nature flat enough to spread the smallest of tea table cloths.

At these picnics the wine is always cool, streams babble unpolluted, the smoked salmon stays moist, its edges uncurled, the raised game pie is as light and fluffy as the clouds, the strawberries glow in the sun, and no one drops beetroot on cool white dresses.

In creating the grand picnic it helps if nothing is synthetic – neither the cream in the coffee nor the plates and cutlery. The French, though they design some of the best plastic camping and picnic equipment in the world, never sacrifice any comforts when eating *al fresco* if the sight of them dining by roadsides in France is to be believed. They sit on chairs at a table, with proper glasses, plates, cutlery, thick linen napkins and an umbrella to shade the food, and eat happily for the statutory 2–3 hours.

A big car boot and willing hands are needed to transport all the comforts of the formal picnic and the hostess can at least pack the foods in lightweight protective modern boxes. But champagne from a paper cup loses some glamour and chain stores do sell cheap glasses.

Because of the extra equipment and arrangement needed for the grand picnic it is as well to have some ready-to-serve *hors d'oeuvres* to hand which can be passed round with an initial drink while the rest of the food is being un-packed.

A bowl of Spanish olives is a good centre-piece to the initial dishes, and olives are also good for flavouring other starters.

Cream Cheese and Olive Bites

4oz/100g cream cheese
1 tablespoon milk
1oz/25g Spanish stuffed green olives, chopped
Salt and pepper
2oz/50g mixed nuts, finely chopped

Blend cream cheese and milk, stir in olives and add seasoning to taste. Form into small balls and roll in the chopped nuts. Chill in refrigerator. Serve on cocktail sticks stuck in a tomato. *(Makes 12–16)*

A small slice of cold Spanish omelette is also a good opener, to serve while people are still wandering around.

Omelette Slices

4 eggs
Salt and pepper
1 tablespoon olive oil
1 small onion, chopped

1 small green pepper, deseeded and chopped
1 thick slice cooked ham, diced
1 medium potato, cooked, peeled and diced
1 clove garlic, crushed
4 Spanish stuffed green olives, sliced

Lightly beat eggs, add salt and pepper and leave on one side. Heat oil in a 8in/20cm pan. Fry all other ingredients together, turning until softened but not coloured. Pour in egg mixture, letting it run all over and through the filling. Cook quickly for about 3 minutes until lightly browned on the under side. Put under a hot grill to cook top. Turn out on plate, leave to become cold, then slice and serve cold.

(*Makes about 25 slices*)

Deep-fried Mushrooms

Serve these with lemon juice and a small bowl of tartare sauce, with toothpicks for dunking. Allow 2oz/50g small button mushrooms per person. Wash and dry mushrooms. Turn in seasoned flour, beaten egg and breadcrumbs. Fry in deep fat (375°F/190°C) until golden brown. Drain on kitchen paper and serve as soon as possible.

Cheese, though it tends to make people a little thirsty, can be moulded into pots like pâté or small rounds to eat off sticks. Mash 4oz/100g Camembert cheese with nearly as much butter, a finely diced onion and some paprika. Mould into rounds and serve with black bread. Or mix 10oz/275g grated cheese with 4oz/100g butter until well blended. Add 1–2 tablespoons brandy or schnapps and stir until smooth. Add cayenne pepper or caraway seeds and serve with pieces of crusty bread.

Pâtés should be not over-rich, but moist in texture. One made with cod's roe is delightful for a summer day.

Cod's Roe Pâté

8oz/225g unsalted butter
1½lb/700g smoked cod's roe
Juice of ½ a lemon
1 teaspoon chilli sauce
Pickled walnuts

Cream the butter in a large mixing bowl. Scrape the cod's roe from the skin very carefully, making sure that none of the skin remains. Slowly combine the roe with the butter, adding the lemon juice and chilli sauce. Chill and decorate with slices of pickled walnut.

Party presentation of an ordinary tin of pâté can be made by scooping out lemon shells and filling with the pâté blended with a special sauce. *(Serves 8)*

Pâté-stuffed Lemons

4 lemons
2 tablespoons cornflour
1 egg
5½oz/160g pâté
1 teaspoon castor sugar
½ teaspoon salt
Pepper
1 teaspoon capers

Halve lemons lengthwise. Scoop out flesh into a sieve over a basin and press out juice. Keep the lemon skins. Add 2 tablespoons lemon juice to ½ pint/150ml of water. Blend cornflour and a little of the liquid together in a saucepan, then add rest of liquid and bring to boil. Stir over a low heat for 2 minutes and then remove. Separate the egg and put yolk into sauce. Add mashed pâté, sugar, salt, a little pepper and some of the capers. Mix well and leave to cool. Whisk egg white until stiff and fold into mixture. Adjust seasoning if necessary. Pile mixture into lemon skins and garnish with remaining capers. *(Serves 4)*

A creamy mushroom purée goes well with crusty bread.

Iced Paprika Cream

6oz/175g button mushrooms
½ clove garlic
1 dessertspoon vegetable oil
5oz/142g carton natural yogurt
5 fl oz/142ml carton soured cream
Lemon juice
Salt and paprika pepper
Chopped parsley

Slice the mushrooms and put a few slices aside for garnish.
Crush the garlic finely. Put the mushrooms and garlic with
the oil into a blender or through a grinder. The mixture
should become a purée. Blend in the yogurt and soured
cream. Add plenty of lemon juice and salt and paprika to
taste. Serve well chilled, garnished with mushroom slices
and a little chopped parsley.   (*Serves 4–6*)

Chilled soups also make a soothing, easy-to-present
starter to the meal.

Apricot Cream Soup

½oz/15g butter
½oz/15g plain flour
1 pint/575ml milk
2 egg yolks
15oz/428g can apricot halves, drained
1 small onion, finely chopped
Salt and pepper
A little curry powder
2 tablespoons single cream

Melt butter and stir in flour, browning to form a roux.
Gradually add milk, stirring all the time. Remove from heat
and stir in egg yolks. Sieve apricots into sauce, add the
onion and simmer for 2–3 minutes. Season very well, adding
a little curry powder to taste. Chill. Add cream before
serving.   (*Serves 4*)

Chilled Cucumber and Mint Soup

1oz/25g butter
1 small sliced onion
2 cucumbers
½ pint/275ml chicken stock
½ pint/275ml coarsely chopped fresh mint (from about a
    dozen stalks)
Scant 1oz/25g flour
½ pint/275ml milk
5 fl oz/142ml carton soured cream
Salt and pepper
Mint sprigs

Melt butter in large saucepan. Fry onion gently until soft.
Peel cucumbers, reserving a little unpeeled for garnish.
Chop and add to onion. Add chicken stock and mint. Cover
and simmer for 20 minutes. Mix flour into a smooth paste
with some of the milk, gradually add to saucepan, then
follow with rest of milk and bring to boil. Cook for about
2 minutes. Cool. Either rub through a sieve or purée in
liquidiser. Add soured cream, reserving a little for garnish.
Adjust seasoning and chill well before serving. Garnish with
slices of cucumber and sprigs of mint.   (*Serves 4*)

Chilled Love Apple Soup

2lb/1kg ripe tomatoes
½ onion
2 heaped teaspoons sugar
2 tablespoons cornflour, blended with 1 tablespoon water
1 pint/75ml chicken stock
2 tablespoons chopped fresh herbs (basil, chives or chervil)
Salt and pepper
5 fl oz/142ml carton soured cream

Slice tomatoes into a pan, add sliced onion and sugar. Cover
and cook on low heat until tomatoes are soft. Rub through
sieve. Stir in blended cornflour and add stock. Rinse out
pan and return soup to it. Cook, stirring, until soup is

smooth. Stir in half the herbs and season to taste. Chill.
To serve whisk in soured cream and sprinkle with rest of
fresh herbs.   (*Serves 4–6*)

NOTE : Love apple is the more romantic, old English name
for tomato.

On a hot summer day, fruit mixed with salad flavourings
can make a good start to a meal, and reduces thirst. Avo-
cados, officially a fruit, can be used as natural containers
for prawns in Curry Sour Cream Sauce (which can also be
served on sliced cucumber) or mixed with grapefruit to make
Avocado Appetiser. Remember to dip avocado in lemon
juice to stop it going brown.

Prawns in Curry Sour Cream Sauce

1oz/25g butter
½ medium onion, finely chopped
1 teaspoon curry powder
4oz/100g peeled prawns
5 fl oz/142ml carton soured cream
Seasoning to taste
½ cucumber
Paprika pepper

Melt butter and soften chopped onion in it. Add curry
powder and cook 1–2 minutes. Add prawns and fry for 1–2
minutes. Cool, then add soured cream and season to taste.
Serve chilled on finely sliced cucumber sprinkled with
paprika pepper.   (*Serves 4*)

Avocado Appetiser

Peel a medium grapefruit and place segments in a bowl
minus the pith. Halve and stone avocado; dip cut surface in
grapefruit juice. Whisk together 2 tablespoons oil, 1
tablespoon vinegar (preferably tarragon), 1 teaspoon
coarsely chopped mint and a pinch of castor sugar. Adjust
seasoning, serve grapefruit on avocado and spoon over
dressing when at the picnic site.   (*Serves 2*)

In place of avocado, ordinary pears can be made into a cooling opener. Dip them in lemon juice as well.

Sweet and Sour Pears

8 pear halves (canned or fresh)
Lettuce leaves
4oz/100g ham
5 fl oz/142ml carton soured cream
1 teaspoon lemon juice
2 tablespoons raisins
Paprika pepper

Arrange pears on a lettuce leaf (hollow side up) in a container. Chop ham finely, add sour cream, lemon juice and raisins. Pile mixture into pear hollows and chill well. Serve sprinkled with paprika pepper.   (*Serves 8*)

Pear and Green Grape Salad

4 ripe pears
6oz/175g cream cheese
4 dessertspoons mayonnaise
Salt, paprika and freshly ground black pepper
12oz/350g green grapes
Watercress
Lettuce

Halve and peel the pears and remove cores with a teaspoon. Mix the cream cheese with the mayonnaise and season to taste. Arrange pear halves, cut side down, on a plate, and coat with cream cheese mixture. Halve and seed the grapes and press on to the pears to cover them. Garnish with watercress or lettuce.   (*Serves 4*)

Chutney Fruit Dip

4oz/100g cream cheese
4 fl oz/112ml soured cream
2 tablespoons apple chutney

2 tablespoons French dressing
6 silverskin onions, chopped
2 teaspoons lemon juice
1lb/500g dessert pears

Mix the cheese with the cream until smooth. Add the apple
chutney, French dressing, onions and lemon juice. Beat
well. Cut the pears into wedges and arrange around the dip.
Serve chilled.   (*Serves 4*)

Main dishes should look as well as taste good. Cold
soufflés, mousses, sauced presentations of fish are all appetising, not over-heavy and easy to eat with spoon or fork
accompanied by rolls, crusty bread or salads. They can be
made and transported in large plastic containers.

Prawn and Cheese Mousse

½oz/15g butter
½oz/15g plain flour
½ pint/275 ml cider
8oz/225g Cheddar cheese, grated
2 eggs, separated
2 level tablespoons tomato ketchup
2 level tablespoons chopped parsley
Salt and pepper
8oz/225g prawns, roughly chopped
½oz/15g powdered gelatine
5 fl oz/142ml double cream

Melt butter, add flour and cook for a minute. Remove from
heat, and gradually stir in cider, reserving 3 tablespoons.
Return to heat and bring to the boil, stirring. Cook for a
minute, remove from heat. Add cheese, egg yolks, tomato
ketchup, parsley and seasoning, and stir until cheese has
melted. Add prawns. Add gelatine to 3 tablespoons cider
and dissolve over a gentle heat. Whip cream until thick but
not stiff and stir into cheese mixture. Add gelatine and mix
in well. Whisk egg whites until stiff and gently fold into

mixture using a metal spoon. Pour into a 2 pint/1·2 litre
mould and put in refrigerator to set.   (*Serves 8*)

Cold Cheese Soufflé

½ pint/275ml milk
1 small onion, peeled and halved
2 sprigs parsley
1 bay leaf
1oz/25g butter
1oz/25g flour
6oz/175g Lancashire cheese, crumbled
¼ level teaspoon made mustard
Salt and pepper
3 eggs, separated
5 fl oz/142ml double cream
2 tablespoons thick mayonnaise
1 tablespoon Worcestershire sauce
½oz/15g gelatine
2 tablespoons water
Peanuts and tomato to garnish

Place milk, onion, parsley and bay leaf in a pan and bring
to boil. Remove from heat and leave to infuse for 10
minutes, then strain. Melt butter in pan, stir in flour and
cook gently for 1 minute. Blend in flavoured milk and
bring to boil, stirring. Cook for 1 minute. Remove from
heat and stir in cheese, mustard and seasoning. Add egg
yolks, one at a time and leave to cool. Prepare a 1 pint/
½ litre soufflé dish with a double strip of greaseproof paper
secured round the outside to form a collar 2in/5cm above
rim. Lightly whip cream and fold into cheese sauce with
mayonnaise and Worcestershire sauce. Dissolve gelatine
in water over pan of hot water, cool and fold into cheese
mixture. Whisk egg whites until just stiff and fold into
cheese mixture. Turn into prepared soufflé dish and chill
until set. Remove paper collar and coat edge of soufflé with
chopped peanuts. Garnish centre with tomato slices. Pack
carefully in larger plastic container or carton.   (*Serves 6–8*)

Gravad Laks or Gravad Halibut (Sugar-cured salmon or halibut – a traditional Scandinavian delicacy)

1 whole fish (about 7–8lb/3½kg)
Handful of sugar
Handful of sea salt
Coarsely ground black pepper
8 tablespoons cognac
Fresh or dried dill and fennel

Divide the fish in two and bone, leaving two fillets – do not skin. Wash each fillet carefully and dry with paper towels so that the flesh is not torn. Mix the sugar, salt, pepper and herbs (if dried) and rub into the surface of the fish. Sprinkle with cognac. Place fresh fennel and dill on the bottom of a large deep pan or ceramic dish (not aluminium) and lay one fillet down. Add more dill and fennel, lay the other fillet on top and add more fennel and dill. Weight the fish with a heavy plate or board. Leave to marinate for 4–5 days in a refrigerator. Remove the marinade and slice finely. Serve with wedges of lemon, Mustard Sauce and cumin bread. (The fish will keep for one week refrigerated.) (*Serves 12*)

Mustard Sauce
Add mustard to a basic béchamel sauce (French white sauce) together with a little sugar and freshly chopped dill.

Meat and poultry should be well presented. A whole ham carved off a wooden board is superb, or a forehock of bacon boned and rolled and easy to slice, can be served with an orange salad.

Bacon with Orange Salad

2½lb/1½kg Danish forehock bacon, boned and rolled
2 bay leaves
1 onion
1 carrot
2 tablespoons toasted breadcrumbs

Put the bacon in a saucepan with plenty of cold water and bring to the boil. Remove from heat, drain off water and cover with fresh cold water. Add bay leaves, peeled onion and carrot. Cover pan and reheat until bacon is just simmering. Simmer the bacon for 20 minutes per 1lb/½kg and 20 minutes over. Remove bacon from pan and wait a few minutes before stripping off the rind. Sprinkle top fat with the breadcrumbs.   (*Serves 4*)

Orange Salad
2 large oranges
1 lettuce
Oil and vinegar
Salt and pepper
Parsley or chives

Peel and slice oranges crossways. Wash and dry lettuce. Mix 2 tablespoons vinegar with 4 tablespoons olive oil. Season with salt and pepper, add freshly chopped parsley or chives. Shake mixture in screw-top jar until it thickens. Pour dressing over oranges and lettuce. Serve at once.

Cold duck goes well with fruit too, but this Iced Fruit Curry can also be served with chicken and other light meats.

Cold Duck and Iced Fruit Curry

2 dessertspoons desiccated coconut
¼ pint/150ml boiling water
2 small onions
2oz/50g butter
2–3 dessertspoons flour
1 level dessertspoon curry powder
1 teaspoon curry paste
1 teaspoon coriander seeds
2 knobs stem ginger, chopped
2 firm pears
2 dessert apples
2 breakfast cups fresh fruit (apricots, pears, plums, melon, mangoes, bananas etc)

2–3 dessertspoons lemon juice
Salt to taste
2½ fl oz/70ml cream
1 cold roast duck

Soak coconut in water for at least 10 minutes. Lightly fry
onions in butter. Add flour, curry powder and paste,
coriander and ginger and continue cooking gently for 5
minutes. Add stock and coconut liquid and simmer for 30
minutes. Peel, core and slice pears and apples. Halve and
stone apricots and plums. Cut melon flesh into chunks, slice
mangoes and bananas. Mix into sauce and cook gently for
5–10 minutes. Blend in cream, add lemon juice and
seasoning to taste. Skin and cut duck into neat pieces and
mix into sauce. Chill thoroughly. Serve in a border of cold
fluffy rice.   (*Serves 6*)

Hand-raised pies – they always sound like petted birds –
were the glory of earlier English picnics on the more
flamboyant scale. This raised pie uses a mixture of bacon
and chicken for its filling.

Raised Pie

10oz/275g collar bacon, finely diced
10oz/275g fresh chicken, finely diced
1 level tablespoon chopped parsley
Grated rind of 1 small lemon
Salt and pepper
A little stock or water
1 egg, hard-boiled
Jelly stock (2 level teaspoons gelatine, ½ pint/275ml chicken
   stock)

Hot water crust pastry
1lb/500g shortcrust pastry mix
8oz/225g plain flour
½ level teaspoon salt
7 fl oz/200ml hot water
Beaten egg

Mix together bacon, chicken, parsley, lemon rind and seasoning. Moisten with a little stock or water. To make pastry prepare as usual for shortcrust, or mix shortcrust pastry mix together in a basin. Bring water to the boil. Pour into the pastry mix, stirring with a wooden spoon to form a ball of dough. When cool enough to handle, knead for 2 minutes until smooth and free from cracks. Roll out two-thirds of the pastry, keeping reserved pastry under a bowl in a warm place. Use pastry to line a 6in/15cm loose-based round cake tin.

Half-fill the pastry case with the meat mixture. Put egg in centre and add remaining meat mixture. Roll out remaining pastry, cover and decorate pie with pastry trimmings. Glaze the top with a little beaten egg. Bake in the centre of a hot oven (425°F/220°C/Gas 7) for 15–20 minutes. Then reduce the heat to moderate (350°F/180°C/Gas 4) and continue cooking for a further 1–1½ hours, or until meat feels tender when tested with a skewer.

When cold fill the pie up with jelly stock made by dissolving gelatine in chicken stock over hot water. Allow to set. (*Serves 6–8*)

Desserts, like many of the suggested main dishes, should be light, whipped up and creamy. After all much of the dignity and graciousness of the grand *fête champêtre* is lost if the tough meat skids off the plate on to a smart outfit or if the dessert has to be bitten hard. It's far easier to loll back on the punt cushions, or lift the binoculars to eye a pleasing young filly – interpret that how you will – while gently spooning up a raspberry fool or fruit mousse. And if romance in a long cotton gown and hat trailing ribbons is the day's setting, a sharing of a spoon-fed dish is so much smoother than trying to cram a crumbling slab of pie down the loved one's gullet!

Citrus Cream

2 oranges
1½oz/40g sultanas
6oz/170g can cream

5oz/142g carton natural yogurt
Cinnamon or nutmeg

Remove the peel and pith from the oranges. Separate the
segments from the skin and place them in a bowl. Add the
sultanas and leave to soak with the oranges. Stir the cream
and yogurt together. Top the fruit with the cream mixture
and sprinkle with cinnamon or nutmeg.   (*Serves 4*)

Cranberry Sherry Mousse

13½oz/390g cranberry jelly
4 tablespoons sherry
10 fl oz/283ml double cream
Chopped walnuts

Put jelly into a basin, add sherry and whisk well together.
Whip the cream, fold into mixture and pile into individual
containers. Decorate with extra cream and nuts. (*Serves 4–6*)

Cider Fool

½ pint/275ml cider
1lb/500g summer fruit
Sugar to sweeten
1½ level tablespoon cornflour
Double cream
Sliced almonds

Simmer the cider and prepared fruit together in a covered
pan until very soft. Rub through a sieve or purée in a
blender. Measure and add enough cider to make up to
3 pints/1¾ litres. Sweeten to taste and reheat. Mix the
cornflour to a smooth paste with cider or water, add to the
fruit and boil while stirring for 3 minutes. Allow to cool,
stirring occasionally. Pour into a container and chill. Serve
topped with sweetened whipped cream and almond spikes.
                                            (*Serves 4–5*)

Strawberry Cheese Ring

1lb/500g curd cheese
2 × 5oz/142g cartons natural yogurt
1oz/25g gelatine
Juice and rind of 2 lemons
2 egg whites, stiffly beaten
½lb/250g fresh strawberries
4oz/100g strawberry jam
A little freshly ground black pepper.

Beat together cheese and yogurt until creamy. Dissolve
gelatine in a little of the lemon juice, over hot water. Fold
into cheese mixture with remaining lemon juice and rind
and the egg whites. Pour into a lightly oiled ring mould and
refrigerate until set (about 2½ hours). Turn out on to a plate
and fill the centre with strawberries. Sprinkle with a little
black pepper – it really does bring out their flavour. Heat
jam in a pan and spoon over the ring. Carry on a plate in
large protective waxed carton.   (*Serves 8*)

Pineapple Crush

2 tablespoons butter
6oz/175g icing sugar
2 egg yolks
3oz/75g crushed cornflakes
8oz/225g pineapple, drained and crushed
1½oz/40g chopped walnuts
5 fl oz/142ml double cream

Cream the butter and icing sugar and beat in the egg yolks.
Fold in half the cornflakes. Mix the crushed pineapple with
the nuts. Spread the butter mixture in the base of a container.
Add the pineapple and sprinkle the remaining crushed
cornflakes on the top. Chill several hours or overnight. Pile
on the cream before serving.   (*Serves 4–6*)

And for a splendid presentation of the best of the British
picnic summer fruits, serve Strawberry Romanoff.

Strawberry Romanoff

1lb/500g strawberries
2–3 tablespoons castor sugar
1 sherry glass medium dry white wine
10 fl oz/283ml double cream

Wash, hull and slice the strawberries, reserving a few for decoration. Put the sliced strawberries in a bowl and sprinkle with castor sugar. Pour over wine and leave for an hour or so, turning the fruit gently a couple of times. Whip the cream until thick. Stir in the strawberry juices and check to see if more sugar is needed. Fold in the strawberries. Turn into serving dishes and decorate with the whole strawberries.   (*Serves 4*)

Or, if you are being greedy, serve a big bowl of unhulled strawberries with a bowl of castor sugar for dunking as the coffee is passed around and picnickers relax and digest.

10
The Wine That Travels Well

Mrs Beeton may seem lavish in her listing of picnic drink, but a basic necessity of any meal outdoors is plenty to drink whether it is lemonade or champagne. The first thing out of the hamper should be a drink, so keep the corkscrew to hand, not buried under everything else.

While champagne and other sparkling wines are ideal for giving a lift to any occasion and can be opened without a corkscrew, they do tend to be shaken up *en route* and care should be taken when opening them so as not to lose any of the precious contents.

Carrying chilled wines to an outdoor meal is a problem. Those zip-round insulated bags with a cold bag in the lid are the best for this. Rigid foam plastic boxes are standard in other countries but are only now catching on in Europe. Taxi drivers in Alice Springs, Australia, for example, carry them full of chilled beer to combat the 'bulldust' of the outback.

Wine decanted into a vacuum flask is fine but seems to lack the appeal of the original bottle. The simplest way, failing other aids, is to take wine bottles, preferably pre-chilled, and wrap them well in newspaper soaked in cold water, then seal the whole in a big plastic bag. Patrick Forbes, director of Moet and Chandon, believes champagne should not be over-chilled or iced, so this method is probably a good way of carrying champagne a short distance.

If you are not going too far you can improvise an ice bucket with ice cubes in a big strong plastic bag in which the wine bottle is set. The whole must be well sealed, or set in a plastic bucket for safety.

A home-made insulated box can be made by lining a plastic bucket with a handle or a bread bin with a lid with foamed polystyrene sheet.

Not all occasions call for cold drinks; winter picnics and sports meetings need something warming in the flask. I made a hit at a god-child's rugger match on a raw February day by providing mulled wine laced with brandy in an innocent-looking vacuum flask for some of the numbed watchers, whose cheering improved markedly after a tumbler-full.

A basic mulled wine recipe, similar to the Glühwein served so welcomingly off the ski slopes in Austria, need not be expensive to make. Use inexpensive red wine and if necessary add to the mixture below, 1 pint/575ml strong black tea or water. Always pre-heat vacuum flasks before filling them with a hot punch.

Glühwein

1 bottle of red wine
4 cloves
½ stick of cinnamon
3oz/75g brown sugar
Rind of ½ a lemon

Place all the ingredients into a pan and heat. Just *before* the mixture reaches boiling point, remove from heat and strain into glasses which have been pre-warmed, or into the vacuum flask.

A variation on this basic punch includes chopped fruit.

Down Under Mulled Wine

1 bottle red wine
1 tablespoon honey
2 tablespoons sugar
Pinch cinnamon
Pinch ginger
8oz/225g can pineapple cubes, chopped
8oz/225g can sliced peaches, chopped
1 large measure brandy
1 pint/575ml hot water

Heat together the wine, honey, sugar and spices. When near to boiling point add pineapple and peaches. Heat for a few seconds further before stirring in brandy and hot water. Serve very hot.   (*Serves 12*)

As a warmer-up to start a picnic on a cold day, Dubonnet can be used with some rum, water and spices to make a glowing drink.

Dubonnet Good Cheer Punch

1 bottle Dubonnet
1½ pints/¾ litre water
Juice of 1 lemon
Strips of pared lemon rind
4 tablespoons dark rum
2½oz/75g sugar
Cardomom seeds
1 lemon, thinly sliced

Blend all the ingredients in a large saucepan with the exception of the lemon slices. (The strips of pared lemon rind and cardomom seeds give a good aroma.) Heat slowly

to near boiling point but do not allow to boil. Add lemon
slices and fill flasks.   (*Serves 8 glasses*)

Punches need not use wine; traditional ale and cider are
fine. Wassail is excellent for a winter walking pause; and
was formerly served to carol singers to keep them warm on
their rounds.

Wassail

1 pint/575ml light ale
½ bottle dry sherry
¼ teaspoon ground nutmeg
½ teaspoon ground cinnamon
¼ teaspoon ground ginger
Sugar to taste
2 small apples

Put the ale, sherry and spices and sugar in a saucepan. Heat
until hot, but do not boil. Keep hot for 15 minutes over a
very low heat, taking care not to let the mixture boil. Pour
into the flask. Peel and slice the apples and add.   (*Serves 6*)

Cider can simply be heated with a small quantity of ginger
or ginger wine, or a little cinnamon and a glass of sherry.
A few cloves can also be added for extra flavour. Another
simple-to-make-brew is a flagon of cider heated with long
strips of the rind of two lemons. Add lemon juice to 2oz/50g
sugar and stir to dissolve. When cider is hot but not boiling
add lemon juice.

This mulled cider cup was created for the revival of was-
sailing in the West Country when in January, on Old Twelfth
Night, farmers wassail the evil spirits from the apple trees
to ensure a good crop.

Mulled Cider Cup

3 flagons dry cider
4 tablespoons brown sugar
2 sliced oranges

4 cloves
¼ teaspoon grated nutmeg
¼ teaspoon grated cinnamon
2 bananas

Heat the cider slowly with the sugar, sliced oranges and
spices until almost boiling. Add the thinly sliced bananas
and serve at once.

(Serves 10)

Tea is of course the traditional, non-alcoholic picnic
drink. Yet it isn't easy to make the perfect cup; too often
it can turn out as a stewed mess. For the freshest tea take
boiling hot water in the flask, then add tea bags on arrival,
ten minutes before the drink is needed, to allow for below-
boiling temperature. Taking plain water also solves the
problem of some wanting coffee, some tea, for instant coffee
can be used. Otherwise take black coffee and, as with tea,
add milk when it's poured. Never pre-mix the milk with
tea or coffee in the flask.

To make the perfect picnic tea preheat the flask by filling
it with hot water, leaving it for a few minutes, then emptying
it out. Prepare the tea as usual in the tea pot and strain it
carefully into the flask; even one or two tea leaves will stew
and spoil the flavour. If the stopper is the old-fashioned cork
type wrap it with greaseproof paper before replacing or it
too will spoil the tea's flavour.

After a picnic rinse the flask with hot water and store it
with the stopper removed to prevent mustiness. If a flask
does smell stale rinse it with a solution of bicarbonate of
soda and warm water. Store the flask with a lump of sugar
in it to keep it sweet.

Various flavours can be added to tea – lemon, of course,
for Russian tea, and sugar to taste. Blackcurrant cordial
makes a good winter warming drink.

CUP WINNERS

The light, slightly *pétillant* green wines, the *vinho verdes* of
Portugal, are ideal with summer meals if kept really cool.

For a grand picnic a Pimms Fizz could start off the meal – and also make the champagne go further. Fill tall glasses with ice, add a measure of Pimms and top up with champagne, lemon slice and cucumber twist (or use pre-chilled Pimms and champagne).

The German Sekt is a lovely light wine for summer, and used with summer fruit it makes an elegant cup for patio parties or grand outdoor spreads.

Sparkling Sekt Summer Cup

8oz/225g mixed summer fruit (strawberries, raspberries
    etc)
2 tablespoons castor sugar
1 bottle Rhine or Moselle wine.
1 bottle Sekt (German sparkling wine)
2 oranges
1 siphon soda water
Mint or borage

Put the washed soft fruits in the bottom of the punch bowl, sprinkle on the sugar and leave for half an hour. Pour the still wine over the fruits and leave, preferably in the refrigerator, for several hours. Add the chilled Sekt, sliced oranges and soda water and fill chilled flasks. Take sprigs of borage or mint to decorate the glasses.   (*Serves 16–18*)

Less expensive sparkle can be added using wines like Café de Paris or champagne cider as a base. *Kir* can be made by adding a half measure of Crème de Cassis (blackcurrant liqueur), well chilled, to the glass of sparkling wine.

Golden Cup

15oz/428g can apricot halves
15oz/428g can peach halves, drained
1 litre bottle of cider
1 2in/5cm stick cinnamon
2 bananas, sliced
1 'split' tonic water

Sieve apricot halves and mix with juice from can. Chop peach halves very finely and add to apricots. Put half the cider into a saucepan with the cinnamon. Bring to the boil. Remove from heat and allow to become cold. Remove cinnamon and add cider to fruit mixture. Stir in remaining cider, bananas and tonic water.　　　　　　　(*Serves 8*)

Blackthorn Cooler

1 tablespoon lime juice cordial
½ pint/275ml dry cider
8½ fl oz/241ml bottle Slim-line bitter lemon
Apple slices
Mint sprig

Put lime juice into a jug. Add cider and bitter lemon. Stir well and add slices of apple and a sprig of mint.　　(*Serves 4*)

Indian Summer Cider

4 teaspoons castor sugar
½ pint/275ml freshly made Indian tea
½ pint/275ml cider
4 slices lemon

Add sugar to tea. Stir until dissolved. Combine with cider. Chill. Add a slice of lemon to each glass.　　　　　(*Serves 4*)

Fair Maid of Hereford

1 pint/575ml cider
½ pint/275ml ginger beer
¼ pint/150ml orange juice
6 sprigs fresh mint

Combine cider with ginger beer and orange juice. Pour into flasks. Add a sprig of mint to each glass on serving.
　　　　　　　　　　　　　　　　　　(*Makes 6–8 glasses*)

The Wine That Travels Well

Sangria is well known by visitors to Spain as a cooling summer cup and travels well to a picnic, the fruit having time to impart its flavour to the wines.

Sangria

1 bottle inexpensive dry red wine
1 bottle plain lemonade
2 tablespoons brandy
1 tablespoon castor sugar
1 orange
1 lemon

Mix together the wine, lemonade, brandy and sugar. Chill and decorate with slices of orange and lemon.

(Makes about 2½ pints / 1½ litres)

Drivers, dieters and children will want a non-alcoholic drink that, just the same, looks festive. Children go for decorated glasses, and sliced orange, cucumber and lemon can be taken along wrapped in foil packs. Small decorative 'kebabs' of cherry, pineapple chunk, cucumber and mint on a cocktail stick can be made up ready to place in a tall glass.

Fruit Cup

Mix a bottle of grape juice with bottle of apple juice and add orange slices.

Summer Punch

Juice of 4 oranges
Juice of 2 lemons
Juice of 1 small grapefruit
1 tablespoon clear honey
2 × 8½ fl oz / 241ml bottles soda water
Few orange segments and slices of fresh summer fruit

Mix together orange, lemon and grapefruit juice, and stir in the honey. Chill for an hour. Add soda water and fruit.

(Serves 4–6)

Cold Fruit Punch

½ pint/275ml strong tea
½ pint/275ml orange juice, unsweetened
¼ pint/150ml lemon juice
½ pint/275ml pineapple juice
1 pint/575ml low-calorie ginger ale
½ pint/275ml water
Sugar to taste
Thin slices orange and lemon

Mix all ingredients except the fruit. Leave in a cold place
for 2–3 hours before serving. Serve garnished with orange
and lemon slices. *(Makes 6 large glasses)*

NOTE: If a ½ teaspoon liquid artificial sweetener is used
instead of sugar this punch has only 53 calories per glass.

Iced tea or coffee make a change on a hot day. As with
other cold drinks carried in a flask, chill the flask by leaving
in the refrigerator overnight. Filled in the morning, it will
stay chilled until lunchtime at least.

To make iced tea, make four times the usual strength
brew of tea and strain into an equal amount of cold water.
Add one dessertspoon fresh lemon juice or unsweetened
bottled lemon. Serve with lemon slice or sprig of mint.
Sweetening should be added in the form of sugar syrup made
by pouring a little hot water on the required amount of
sugar (or use liquid artificial sweetener).

Coffee, too, needs to be double strength to face dilution
with ice. Iced coffee can be made quickly by using two coffee
bags per person. Chill freshly brewed double strength coffee
in enamel, pottery or glass jug (metal imparts flavour) and
do not keep for more than a few hours as its freshness fades.
Add cream and sugar to taste on serving. Or add a measure
of Crème de Cacao liqueur for lift, when less sugar will be
needed.

Index

147

Index

148

Index

Index

Index